A beautiful Easter scene dating from 18th April 1981. The **Manx Maid** *is alongside in the "North Edward" pier berth whilst the* **Ben-my-Chree** *is seen arriving from Liverpool. The "Ben" had covered two Dublin sailings the day before. The* **Lady of Mann** *was also in service. In the foreground, recreational grass on Douglas Head spreads out before the camera and to the left is the green shelter which, until its demolition a few years ago, was to feature on so many photographs of Douglas Head. In the middle distance is the grand sweep of Douglas Bay, its guest houses and hotels that owe their charming facades to Victorian planners and architects of over a century ago.*
That spring, the **Mona's Queen** *had been to Govan on the Clyde for her overhaul and did not emerge until after Easter.* *(photo: Author)*

(inside front cover)

The **Lady of Mann** *heads for the Isle of Man in westerly gales on 21st February 1995 under the command of the fleet commodore, Capt. E.C. (Edward) Fargher. The combination of the gale and high tide was such that, upon leaving Heysham, Capt. Fargher decided to go astern from the quay all the way down the harbour, and only when well clear of the "roundheads" marking the physical outer limit of Port of Heysham, did he swing the ship and set course for the rough trip to Douglas.*

During the voyage the weather continued to deteriorate and by the time the author took this photograph, the **Lady of Mann** *was ploughing head on, into very heavy seas. It was bitterly cold and, the gale having risen still further, was howling in the stays and halyards. To remain standing up was virtually impossible and water and spray were flying everywhere.*

At a little over half way into the voyage, Capt. Fargher addressed passengers on the loudspeaker system and apologised that as the weather had become far worse than was forecast and on account of the heavy seas the ship was now encountering, he was now going to have to slow down. Almost imperceptibly, the "Lady's" main engine revolutions began to die away thus affording ship and passengers a little respite from the pounding they had endured. As the ship gained the lee of the Island's land mass, the seas gradually became less severe and passenger comfort and composure were soon restored.

Despite the conditions, the **Lady of Mann** *docked at Douglas no more than thirty minutes late having done everything that was required of her bringing her passengers safely home through the gale.*

(photo: Author)

(front cover)

The **Manx Maid** *at Sea. From a watercolour by John H. Nicholson in the author's collection of original paintings by local artists.*

(back cover)

The **Mona's Queen** *off Douglas. From a watercolour by John H. Nicholson in the author's collection of original paintings by local artists.*

Contents

So Strong And So Fair

The story of the side-loading car ferries of the Isle of Man Steam Packet Company and their people

by Richard Danielson

Published by Maritime Publications, Laxey, Isle of Man, IM4 7JT.

Text origination and design by The Creative Studio Limited, Fort Street, Douglas, Isle of Man.
Printed by Nelson Press Co. Limited, Kingswood Grove, Douglas, Isle of Man.

ISBN 0 9513155 9 5

Introduction

There is something very special, even magical, about the sea voyage to the Isle of Man. It is difficult to define yet once experienced, immediately elevates the heart and mind to thoughts of what lies four hours steaming time ahead. Such things as home, family life, safety, comfort and belonging.
Battling its way to Douglas, the Isle of Man boat is really quite small, yet it is a powerful, even brave manifestation of the best that is Manx. Overnight voyages and those in storms, for which the capricious Irish Sea is renown, also add a further dimension of respect for ones existence and faith that whatever happens in the next few hours, one will arrive safely at journey's end.
And just what is at journey's end?

Journey's end. *First glimpse of the Island when the ship is still anything up to an hour off Douglas. Ancient mariners used to say this was "atterrage", that is to say literally, to make land.*
(photo: Author)

The Isle of Man is more that just one of the most beautiful places in the world – much more. Constitutionally, the Island is "a self governing crown dependency" but is probably better known to most people for its tail-less cats, Manx kippers and the world renown T.T. motorcycle races. Whether the Island is somewhere to enjoy a lovely holiday or whether it is home, here one can be alone in the hills and glens or happy amongst groups of like minded people. One can live in town houses that once belonged to another era but now, tastefully renovated, make wonderful family homes; or in something much newer. Large dwellings and isolated country cottages, mansions and farmhouses all abound. In the towns and villages there is cultural activity at all levels. The Island has its own laws, postage stamps, money, low taxes, Manx Gaelic language and a folklore involving little people and fairies. The latter not to be confused with the local saying "He's away with the fairies" meaning that the subject is probably a little simple.
The Isle of Man's history is longer than most yet it is a forward not backward looking, independent nation. Independent yes, but certainly not unapproachable. Its borders are well and truly open to all who come with good intent. And if one stays a while, one quickly adapts to the Island's calmer way of life. Driving the length or breadth of the Island will soon take on the proportions of a major travelogue requiring a prior good night's sleep, a hearty breakfast and break for lunch if the journey is to be accomplished comfortably. It should be pointed out that the Island measures just over thirty miles from end to end but there is a tremendous amount of beautiful space and peace in between!
In any context other than the Manx National Anthem from where they have been taken, it would only be appropriate to use these five special words – *So Strong and so Fair* - to describe something so notable as to warrant its recognition as being really important to us all. The author believes that this honour rightfully belongs to the subjects of this book.
This then is the story of the the four passenger car ferries of the Isle of Man Steam Packet Company's fleet and of some of the people connected with them. In the end, in some circles these ships became virtually nameless and known simply as "the side-loaders". In the following pages, with the help of others, the author hopes to confirm that these handsome ships were quite exceptional in their historic importance to the Island's whole economy and way of life.
The author's previous works have dealt with most of the other past and present ships of the Steam Packet fleet and therefore this book provides brief details of other vessels sufficient only to facilitate recognition of the actual events in question.
The ships upon which this book concentrates, are those named ***Manx Maid*** (1962), ***Ben-my-Chree*** (1966), ***Mona's Queen*** (1972) and ***Lady of Mann*** (1976). The personalities are just some of the hundreds that have helped to make the Isle of Man Steam Packet Company a truly fine institution.
These four Manx ships were very skilfully designed and provided the most versatile means ever known of carrying large numbers of passengers in comfort, together with their cars which could be loaded at all states of the tide from any harbour or dock wall capable of accommodating the stern quarter of the ship. They needed virtually no shore based equipment nor expensive linkspans to enable them to pick up their payload. Perhaps this is just as well because, as we shall see later, very few of the destinations they served originally had any such equipment. Not for them the laboriously slow, mechanical and hydraulic vehicle hoists being introduced on the new Clyde ferries, nor was the Isle of Man going to emulate the rather unsophisticated conversion of old cross Channel steamers as had occurred elsewhere.
On 29th March 1996, when production of this book – *So Strong and So Fair* – was nearing completion, the news of Sea Containers' take-over of the Steam Packet Company was announced. The opportunity has therefore also been taken to pay tribute to the ***Peveril***, the Company's first roll on-roll off ship.

In the Beginning

The immediate scene for this book is set shortly before Christmas in 1959 at which time the Isle of Man Steam Packet Company Limited through its directors, managers and their marine and engineering superintendents set about determining the precise specifications for the company's first car ferry.
In order to put matters further in perspective it is first necessary to remember (or imagine) what travel to the island was like before the advent of the car ferries. In an earlier book by the author entitled *The Isle of Man Steam Packet Volume 2*, there is quoted in full the relevant parts of a letter in the author's possession dated 16th May 1932 from the Steam Packet Company's marine superintendent to its general manager on the subject of transporting vehicles by sea to the Island. The opening sentence of that letter reads as follows:
"The question of conveying motor cars by the passenger steamers has received my earnest and careful consideration for some years and whilst every inducement is given to passengers to travel with their cars, I cannot however, recommend any departure from our present regulations viz., that cars by passenger steamer be carried only by special arrangement".
He then went on to spell out the thought processes that had led him to that conclusion.

THE ISLE OF MAN STEAM PACKET COMPANY LIMITED

(Incorporated in the Isle of Man)

Passengers' Unaccompanied Cars by Cargo Vessels.

Attention is drawn to the fact that passengers travelling by the Company's services can have their cars conveyed at a **reduced rate for the return journey** providing the car is conveyed **both ways** by the **cargo service** between Liverpool and Douglas, within three months.

The following table shows the cost of the return journey—

Overall Length (Bumper to Bumper and as shown by the car manufacturers in their lists of specifications)—	Outward journey £ s. d.	Homeward journey £ s. d.	Total cost £ s. d.
Under 9 ft. 6 ins.	1 19 0	18 9	2 17 9
under 10 ft. 6 ins.	3 2 6	1 10 0	4 12 6
under 11 ft. 6 ins.	4 4 6	2 0 6	6 5 0
under 12 ft. 6 ins.	5 12 0	2 14 0	8 6 0
under 13 ft. 6 ins.	6 3 0	2 18 9	9 1 9
under 14 ft. 6 ins.	6 14 0	3 3 6	9 17 6
under 15 ft. 6 ins.	7 5 0	3 8 3	10 13 3
under 16 ft. 6 ins.	8 7 0	3 17 9	12 4 9
16 ft. 6 ins and over	On Application.		

To obtain reduction on homeward journey the outward receipt and the return portion of the passenger ticket must be produced.

Dual-purpose vehicles of the shooting-brake or estate car type, including Land Rovers, jeeps and light vans are accepted as private cars provided they are licensed and insured as such.

SPECIAL REGULATIONS GOVERNING THE CONVEYANCE OF ALL MOTOR VEHICLES BY PASSENGER AND CARGO VESSELS.

Motor Cars will not be shipped unless the Company's form of consignment note is completed by the Owner/Driver, giving full particulars as required thereon, including make of car, registration number and overall length of the vehicle.

Only sufficient petrol to enable a vehicle to be driven on and off the vessel and to the nearest garage may remain in the tank during shipment.

Personal luggage only (within limits allowed) carried free.

Passenger Fares: Liverpool and Douglas.

SINGLE	FIRST CLASS 35/-	SECOND CLASS 27/-
RETURN (3 Months)	FIRST CLASS 60/-	SECOND CLASS 50/-

MID-WEEK: FIRST CLASS 50/-; SECOND CLASS 40/-

These tickets will be available for travel outwards on Tuesday, Wednesday or Thursday and return on either Tuesday, Wednesday or Thursday within a period of three months.

CHILDREN under 3 years of age, FREE; 3 years and under 14, HALF-FARE

Infants must be accompanied by an adult.

Passengers and their accompanied luggage will only be carried subject to the Company's Standard Conditions of Carriage of Passengers and Passengers Accompanied Property as exhibited in the Company's Offices and on board its vessels.

Acceptance of a ticket issued by the Company binds the passenger to these conditions.

AGENTS: **THOS. ORFORD & SON, INDIA BUILDINGS, 40 BRUNSWICK STREET, LIVERPOOL, 2.** Tel.: Central 3214.

A. J. FICK
General Manager

Imperial Buildings,
Douglas, January, 1962

Above: Passengers unaccompanied cars by Cargo Vessels – dated 1962.
(archive material: Author's collection)

DEPARTMENT OF AGRICULTURE AND FISHERIES
FOR SCOTLAND

Postage on any reply to this letter should be prepaid

Maritime House,
LEITH.
EDINBURGH.6.
9th September 1963.

The Marine Superintendent,
Isle of Man Steam Packet Co; Ltd;
Imperial Buildings,
DOUGLAS,
ISLE OF MAN.

Dear Sir,

" MANX MAID "
VEHEELE LASHINGS.

I have read with much interest the information on your " MANX MAID " which has been given in various Journals, and, as I have an interest in Car Ferries now building for service on the West Coast of Scotland, I would appreciate any information you may feel disposed to give on the type of Car lashing you have found to be most efficient and speedy of connection and dis-connection.

The vessels in which I am interested are on the general lines of " MANX MAID " with an extensive garage deck loaded from a vehicle lift at the fore end. Two lanes of cars would be stowed port side and three lanes starboard side, and vehicles would be on board four hours with rough crossings expected at times.

If you could offer detail of the type of car lashing used, and Trade name and suppliers of any patented quick release gear you have found to be satisfactory, I would be extremely grateful to you.

Yours faithfully,
for D.T.MACCALLUM.
Marine superintendent.

When the Steam Packet Company moved from its old Imperial Hotel headquarters by the former Red Quay near the swing bridge in 1969, large quantities of historic data was simply dumped and lost for all time. Fortunately, when marine superintendent Capt. C.H. (Harvey) Collister was moving offices some time later, he had the foresight to hand over to the author, all sorts of items and documents of interest, in order that they at least would be saved. Amongst them was this interesting letter, dated 9th September 1963 linking the successful design of the **Manx Maid** *with the Scottish ferries* **Clansman**, **Columba** *and* **Hebrides**, *then under construction for service to the western isles.*

What a lovely spectacle the **Ben-my-Chree** *makes as Captain Harry Kinley takes her out from Douglas on the morning of 2nd August 1972. He is to be seen on the starboard bridge wing with the second officer, whilst his chief officer is right in the fo'c'sle by the jack staff and the carpenter responsible for the securing the bow rudder is to be seen above the "N" of Ben. Captain Harry Kinley went astern right round to the far side of H.M. Yacht* **Britannia** *where he saluted Her Majesty and received a hearty wave in response.*
Surely the word cynosure was created especially for this scene! The whole island declared a public holiday that day and as the Queen drove all round the island, slowing up at every gathering of well-wishers, she received the warmest of all welcomes.
(photo: Capt. Harry Kinley collection)

As an alternative to vehicles being carried on the old passenger ships, the Steam Packet Company offered large incentives to drivers who were willing to suffer the inconvenience of shipping their cars by cargo boat. The unaccompanied car travelled by sea from the Company's Coburg Dock cargo berth in Liverpool's south docks, whilst the driver and his passengers made their way to the Princes Landing Stage and crossed on the scheduled passenger steamer. This service was still offered as late as 1962, the year when the ***Manx Maid,*** the first car ferry, was introduced.
Before the delivery of the first drive on – drive off Manx car ferry, passengers' cars and motorcycles for shipment by passenger steamer (which in say 1961 numbered over 10,000 cars per year) had to be loaded by driving them aboard over gangplanks when tidal conditions rendered ship and shore more or less level or by crane and sling at other states of the tide. The procedure was time consuming for passengers and crews and with the exception of a small number of traditionalists, was regarded as being more than a little inconvenient for all concerned.
Before loading vehicles on the shelter deck, movable seating constructed of long varnished wooden slatted sections, had to be unclipped and stowed out of the way along with rubbish receptacles and other encumbrances that would otherwise be on deck. When the deck was cleared it enabled about twenty private cars to be carried (forty on the old ***Lady of Mann***) with the attendant nuisance of their taking up valuable covered deck space. After the voyage, everything had to be replaced. But the carriage of cars was an important and fast growing part of the business and could not be ignored. "We were putting them everywhere" said Captain J.E. (Jack) Ronan referring to the cars. "We simply could not go on without having a proper means of dealing with the growing numbers of cars on offer" At sea, freight is always referred to as being "offered".
Being crane loaded onto a ferry required the car owner to drive into the prescribed area beneath the crane jib and cable where a sling comprising a steel frame, onto which were attached two pairs of wooden boards, would be waiting. The driver was required to get out of the car and join the ship by walking down the stone pier steps and across a gangway. The sling's wooden boards would then be positioned so that when the lift began, each pair became a snug fit holding the lower halves of the front and back wheels thus stopping any tendency for the car to roll away. As soon as the car was hoisted up and onto the deck, the driver would be asked to park it in the space indicated. Discharging by crane, which was the opposite procedure, could also take well over an hour, sometimes nearer two. Motorcycles were craned on and off the ships in slings, a few at a time, much to the consternation of their owners including some well known race aces who feared the worst for their beloved machines. *Captain Harry Kinley has more to say on this subject in his memoirs starting on page 68.*

The carriage of light deck cargo aboard ships that were essentially passenger steamers had always been commonplace amongst short sea operators and with the advent of the private car at the beginning of the century and its increasing popularity, there grew up a healthy competition for deck space.

This scene is June 1975 with the crane busily canting over the harbour wall loading motor-cycles during the busy T.T. period.
(photo: Capt. A.W.G. Kissack)

The construction and survey rules for passenger carrying vessels dealt with the matter quite precisely and depending on the type of sea crossing and the passenger certificate to be allocated, specific *volumes* of space below deck and *area* of space above deck had to be provided for each passenger. It is perhaps surprising that persons were not necessarily entitled to a seat but to defined amounts of space on which to stand or, for the lucky few, lie down.

Therefore on ferries designed principally for the carriage of passengers, there were often to be found brass plates in strategic positions throughout the vessel, stipulating the effect on permitted passenger numbers when cargo was being carried. For example, the foc's'le on the post war Manx passenger ferries ***King Orry, Mona's Queen, Tynwald, Snaefell, Mona's Isle*** and ***Manxman*** was originally certified for carrying up to 90 passengers only when not occupied by livestock or other cargo.

This photograph was taken at the end of August 1982. Here we see the **Manxman** *at Douglas already loaded with cars and ready to depart to Belfast on her last ever sailing to Ulster before being sold out of service. Captain Fargher was master for the day, putting time in to maintain his Belfast Harbour pilots licence.*

(photo: Author)

PARCELS TRAFFIC RATES

BY DIRECT PASSENGER VESSEL BETWEEN

LIVERPOOL AND DOUGLAS

(These rates do not include Collection or Delivery or Port Dues when applicable)

STANDARD PARCELS SCALE GROUP 1.

1 to 15 lbs.	1/ 8
16 to 18 lbs.	2/ 2
19 to 20 lbs.	2/ 3
21 to 22 lbs	2/ 5
23 to 24 lbs.	2/ 6
25 to 26 lbs.	2/ 9
27 to 28 lbs.	2/11

Parcels above 28 lbs. to be charged 11/8 per cwt.

Fractions of a penny to be charged as a penny.

STANDARD PARCELS SCALE GROUP 2.

1 to 3 lbs.	1/ 8
4 to 6 lbs.	2/ 2
7 to 10 lbs.	2/ 6
11 to 15 lbs.	3/ 6
16 to 20 lbs.	4/ 5
21 to 24 lbs.	5/ 1
25 to 28 lbs.	5/10

Parcels above 28 lbs. to be charged 23/4 per cwt.

Fractions of a penny to be charged as a penny.

PORTERAGE:—Any Parcel or Package weighing over ½ cwt. will be charged extra for porterage (loading and discharging) as follows:—
57 lbs. to 112 lbs. ...... 5d. per package.
113 lbs. to 168 lbs. ...... 10d. per package.
169 lbs. to 224 lbs. ...... 1/8 per package.

Or 2-3rds of these charges per package if only one of the above services performed by the Company.

DELIVERY in Douglas:
5d. per Parcel up to 28 lbs.
7d. per Parcel 29 lbs. to 56 lbs.
10d. per Parcel 57 lbs. to 112 lbs.

Also certain districts in Onchan:
7d. per Parcel up to 28 lbs.
10d. per Parcel 29 lbs. to 56 lbs.
1/1 per Parcel 57 lbs. to 112 lbs.

BICYCLES, etc (UNACCOMPANIED) (includes Porterage).

Bicycle	11/-	... ...	9/5
Tandem Bicycle or Tricycle	15/8	Perambulator	15/8
Bath Chair	14/3	Auto Cycle	22/3
		Motor Cycle	42/6
		Motor Cycle Combination	42/6
		Motorised Invalid Chair ...	

TRAVELLERS' SAMPLES:—Passenger holding 1st Class ticket, free allowance up to 3 cwt.; if holding 2nd Class ticket, free allowance up to 1½ cwt. Excess is 6/- per cwt.

Passengers' unaccompanied Luggage, Goods, Live Stock, Vehicles, etc., are only conveyed on the Standard Conditions of Carriage as set out in the Company's consignment notes and/or receipts and/or Bills of Lading as the case may be, copies of which as applicable to the particular class of traffic can be obtained from the Offices of the Company or its Agents.

FOR FURTHER PARTICULARS APPLY TO:—
LIVERPOOL—Thos. Orford & Son, India Buildings, 40 Brunswick Street, or Parcels Office, South-East Corner Princes Dock. (Telephone Central 3214).
DOUGLAS—A. C. DOUGLAS, General Manager, Imperial Buildings (Telephone 1101).

February 4th, 1957.

Victoria Press Limited, Douglas.

FREIGHT CHARGES &c., FOR TRAFFIC CARRIED ON STEAMERS DECK

and at Owner's Risk. These Charges do not include Loading and Discharging, which is to be done by the Owner, or Port Dues when applicable.

Live Stock.

DOUGLAS TO LIVERPOOL, OR VICE VERSA.

BULLS		46/10
CALVES (not exceeding 1 month old)		12/10
„ (over 1 month old)		16/1
CATTLE (Dealers)		35/11
„ (Not Dealers)		41/1
DOGS		10/11
DONKEYS		24/5
GOATS		8/4
HORSES (Dealers), Single		70/7
„ „ Two or more	each	64/2
„ (Not Dealers)		76/4
„ STALLIONS		94/4
„ „ Two or more	each	82/6
„ PONIES (12 hands and under), dealers		56/6
„ „ (12 hands and under), not dealers		62/3
„ „ (Shetland)		29/6
„ MULES (Same as Ponies)		
PIGS (Bacon)		13/10
„ (Pork)		11/7
„ (Young) in crate	per ton	83/5
„ in Crates	per cwt.	7/8
SHEEP AND LAMBS		6/2

Liverpool, Fleetwood and Douglas.

BUTTER, CREAM and LIQUID EGG—128/4 per ton (minimum 1 cwt).
CRABS and LOBSTERS—5/9 per cwt.
DRUGS—6/5 per cwt., minimum 1/2.
ESCALLOPS—5/9 per cwt. (minimum 1 cwt.)
FISH (FRESH)—IMPORTED into the ISLE of MAN, 80/10 per ton; **Exported** from the ISLE of MAN, 77/- per ton.
FISH (SALT)—77/- per ton.
FLOWERS and PLANTS, in pots or boxes, 112/4 per ton.
FOWLS, POULTRY and GAME—Live in crates, per cwt. 8/9; Dead in Crates, per cwt. 6/9.
FRUIT and VEGETABLES— 64/2 per ton.
ICE—Packed in bags or wrappers (passenger steamer) 70/7 per ton.
KIPPERS, Smoked or Dried HADDIES and FILLETS, etc.,—83/4 per ton (minimum 1 cwt.); Small Boxes 10d. each.
MEAT—Passenger Steamer, 94/2 per ton.
MERCHANDISE, ACCOMPANIED—7/9 per cwt.
MILK (FRESH)—2½d. gallon (including dues). Returned Empty Cans 3½d. each.
NEWSPAPERS—5/9 per cwt., minimum 1/-.
OYSTERS—5/2 per cwt.
PASSENGERS' ACCOMPANIED LUGGAGE—Passenger holding 1st Class ticket, free allowance up to 150 lbs.; 3rd Class ticket, free allowance 100 lbs. Excess 6/- per cwt.
RABBITS (DEAD)—109/1 per ton (minimum 1 cwt.)

(archive material: Author's collection)

It was quite common for parcels, foodstuffs, furniture, bathroom and kitchen equipment and anything light enough to be carried on and off by hand to be transported on decks of the passenger steamers. This method of transporting goods was widely used and carried on long after the advent of the car ferries. In fact it was only as a result of the proliferation of couriers and door-to-door carriers who could pick up and deliver anywhere (and track the progress of goods by computer and bar-codes) that the "goods carried on deck" service was finally made redundant. Special tariffs were published for the purpose and two are reproduced above.

Companies such as A. Skillicorn Ltd. the famous bathroom and kitchen specialist from Laxey (the author's home village for the last twenty-five years) and many others all used the service fully. We shall have the opportunity to read more of this later.

To quote from the Steam Packet Company's timetables and handbills of almost forty years ago "A limited number of motorcars are conveyed by passenger vessels between Liverpool and Douglas, Fleetwood and Douglas and Ardrossan and Douglas by prior arrangement. Reservation of space must be made at Head office, Douglas or with the Company's Agent at Liverpool (Thomas Orford & Son), Fleetwood (A.D. Morgan, Dock Manager) or Ardrossan (Rennie & Watson, Glasgow). Motor vehicles must be available for loading at least two hours before the advertised sailing time. Vehicle drivers are required to hold a First Class ticket".

At that time, no vehicles of any description were carried to Dublin, Heysham or Llandudno whilst the Belfast service carried solo motorcycles but no combinations or cars. Gradually, the car carrying service was extended using the passenger boats but even as late as 1972 with three car ferries in service, it was still not possible to take a car to Dublin where only solo motorcycles could be carried, nor to Fleetwood which was by then reopened, but no longer carried any vehicles at all.

This photograph shows Lowey's removal van attending the **Manx Maid** *at Liverpool with a load of goods destined for Island traders.*
(photo: Author)

In this wonderfully busy scene, we see the old **Lady of Mann** *arriving at Douglas from Liverpool in June 1970. The Harbour Board crane and sling are ready for action as are the trucks standing by. Readers may still remember the loudspeaker system that was used to announce the arrival of all steamers at Douglas. "The steamer now arriving at the Victoria Pier is the 11 o'clock sailing from Liverpool. The return sailing at 4 o'clock this afternoon is from the Edward Pier and not from this, the Victoria Pier". For a modest tip, porters with handcarts were available to carry suitcases too!*

(photo: George Danielson)

This excellent photograph by well respected transport photographer Norman Jones is of the **Snaefell** *at Liverpool on 16th July 1962. Up these gangplanks, known as the "boards", were driven cars for shipment on the old passenger boats. Likewise, every item of deck cargo, of which there was plenty, was manhandled aboard this way.*

(photo: Norman Jones)

At Liverpool, where the Princes Landing Stage ensured that the height between ship and stage, both of which were floating, was constant, a fair gradient had to be negotiated in order to drive up the unprotected gangplanks followed by a sharp turn onto the shelter deck of the ferry. This task was not always appreciated by the inexperienced or faint hearted. Even after the advent of the fourth car ferry, especially at busy periods, cars were from time to time still carried on the decks of the old passenger steamers. In recent living memory, when craneage was necessary at Douglas it was provided by the Isle of Man Harbour Board mobile crane at the risk of drivers but latterly at the expense of the Steam Packet Company. In earlier times the Steam Packet Company had their own hand powered crane.

The first of the Manx car ferries, the ***Manx Maid,*** was delivered from Cammell Laird & Co (Shipbuilders and Engineers) Limited, in 1962. At that time there were no stern loading linkspan facilities at Douglas (or Peel, the Island's emergency west coast port) nor Liverpool which was at the very centre of the Steam Packet catchment area where the famous floating Princes Landing Stage provided a riverside berth that dictated side loading only.

Elsewhere around the north Irish Sea there were only linkspans at Stranraer, Preston and Larne none of which were Steam Packet destinations under normal circumstances. British Railways had at that time recently renewed its three ship fleet serving Belfast from Heysham but had built large, handsome but quite obsolete passenger ships upon which all freight and vehicles had to be crane loaded. Things were not greatly different at Holyhead and Fishguard serving the Irish Republic, where the drive on – drive off concept was still several years off. So, when that all important decision to seriously consider building a car ferry was taken by the directors of the Isle of Man Steam Packet Company in 1959, it was for a brand new, state of the art ship that would employ all the best thinking by the cream of Britain's naval architects and shipbuilding experts. There was no compromise nor mediocrity in the building of this new ship.

The specification dictated that she is was to be a handsome hybrid, developed from the experience of one hundred and thirty years of passenger ship operation and the emerging need to be able to carry large numbers of cars to and from ports with no vehicle loading facilities.

Right: Captain A.W.G. (Westby) Kissack, aboard the ***Mona's Queen.***

RULES AND REGULATIONS FOR CAPTAINS, OFFICERS, ENGINEERS AND STEWARDS

RULE 4. The utmost courtesy and attention must at all times be shown to passengers whilst on board the company's steamers and the captain shall see that this regulation is observed by the officers and others serving under him and that the comfort of all classes of passengers is disturbed as little as possible by the crew whilst occupied in the working and necessary cleaning of the ships. No swearing or other improper language by any Officer or other member of the crew will be permitted.

RULE 8. No servant is allowed to solicit gratuities from passengers or other persons.

RULE 18. All matters of business connected with the company must be treated as confidential and conversations with passengers on such subjects should be avoided.

RULE 105. Should any passenger behave in an objectionable manner, the steward must at once report the same to the captain.

The car carrying capability was derived from a spiral ramp system built at the stern of the ship which permitted cars (of which over eighty could be carried) motorcycles and vans to enter or leave the vehicle deck with consummate ease, making their final exit off the ship via a simple portable (latterly aluminium) ramp between ship and shore. They also had hydraulically operated doors forward on the main deck for use when the ship was alongside the floating landing stage at Liverpool. Not surprisingly these became known as the "Liverpool Doors".
Deck cargo on the car ferries was still to be manhandled aboard necessitating a long walk down the ramps to the car deck where goods for shipment were stowed.
Under extreme low tide conditions, the portable ramp could be brought inboard so that vehicle disembarkation could continue even when the highest level of the spiral ramp was below the dock wall.
By the autumn of 1973 the car ferries numbered three and, perhaps rather surprisingly, a fourth ship of the same basic design was under consideration for construction and final delivery, supposedly in time for the 1976 T.T.

The spiral loading ramp system of the side-loading car ferries. *(archive material: Author's collection)*

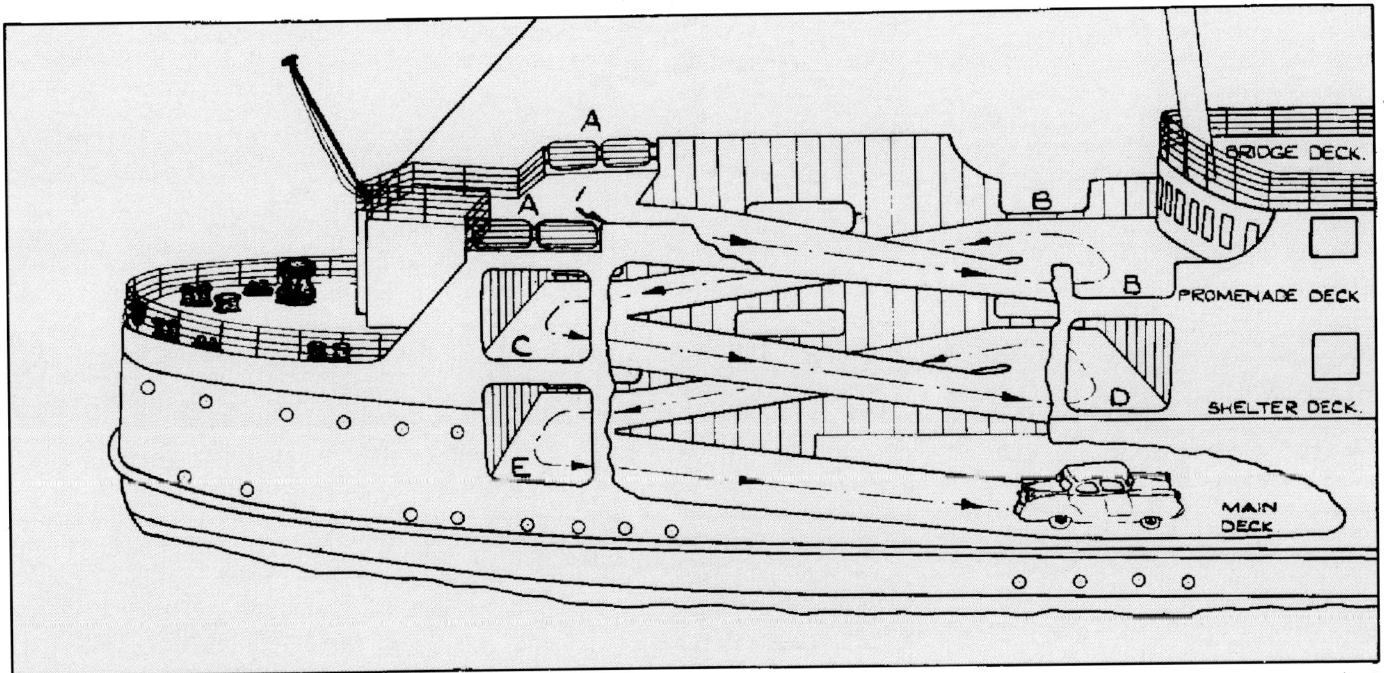

ILLUSTRATING VEHICLE RAMP WITH 5 ACCESS LEVELS TO COVER A TIDAL RANGE OF MORE THAN 20'-0"

"A" TOP ACCESS P & S. REMOVABLE RAILS

"B" PROMENADE DK. ACCESS P & S. SLIDING DOORS.

"C" SHELTER DK. UPPER ACCESS P & S. SLIDING DOORS.

"D" SHELTER DK. LOWER ACCESS P & S SLIDING DOORS

"E" MAIN DK. ACCESS P & S. HINGED DOORS. HYDRAULICALLY OPERATED.

The car ferries were only ever designed to carry passengers and their cars, motorcycles and vans. They had a vehicle deck weight limitation and a height restriction of approximately two metres (6'6"). Other than small vans which description included Transit type vans etc., they could not carry any commercial vehicles, coaches, lorries, containers or trailers. If the car ferries had a downfall, this was certainly it.

By this time all around Britain, the roll on-roll off and container revolution was well underway and many harbours (but still not those in the Isle of Man nor in the river at Liverpool) had a linkspan.

Any large items for transportation to the Island therefore had to be carried aboard one of the separate fleets of cargo boats, with the exception that one bus or coach per voyage could be carried on the fo'c'sle of the old passenger boats. In fact the Company made a lot of publicity out of the fact that, for the sake of their passengers who might otherwise be inconvenienced or delayed, they had no intention of mixing passengers and freight.

Therefore, pursuant to that policy and in the continuing absence of a linkspan at Douglas, the fourth and last passenger car ferry was ordered at a time when it might have been expected that a roll on-roll off multipurpose (combined passenger and freight) ship was appropriate. With the wisdom of hindsight, blessed with which we all have remarkably good, if not perfect vision, the correctness of that decision is a matter for debate beyond the scope of this book.

What is relevant here is that the ***Lady of Mann***, the final passenger car ferry, was built and (following unexpected reprieve at the end of 1995) of the original famous quartet, she alone remains in Manx service.

Top: The **Lady of Mann.** *Above: The* **Manx Maid.** *(photos: Author)*

Top: The **Mona's Queen.** *Above: The* **Ben-my-Chree.** *(photos: Author)*

The four ships of the class were all especially designed for the traditional Isle of Man trade and only rarely were they to be found working elsewhere. On the occasions that they did find charters outside the normal Isle of Man routes, their flexibility, speed and efficiency rightly elicited high praise. In all the author's previous books about the Steam Packet Company, one about the famous Mersey Ferries and a series about Britain's favourite cross channel steamers excursion ships and ferries, specifications of ships was given in minute detail as to technical facts length, breadth and precise horsepower etc.

As far as *So Strong and so Fair* is concerned, this work is rather different. Remembering the maxim, that *"One picture is worth ten thousand words"* this book will rely on well over two hundred photographs and illustrations to tell its story, with the minimum of unnecessary detail.

Throughout the many years of his involvement, it has been the author's privilege to know personally many of the masters, officers and crews of the ships of the Steam Packet Company and some of their wives and families. The directors, managers and superintendents, not least the present incumbents, have always been very approachable and in return, particularly in the 1970s and 1980s, the author was able to reciprocate by functioning as unofficial company photographer and honorary publicity officer.

Therefore, whilst many of the author's photographs found their way onto company postcards, timetables, brochures, calendars and the like, they have also featured on Manx Telecom Phonecards and have been the inspiration for postage stamps too.

"You really should be on the payroll was often said", and that was indeed an honour.

Ships' Officers 1962

This list of masters, navigating and engineering officers for 1962 has been compiled from the sailing sheets, diaries, other records and official lists in the author's possession. To produce such lists is difficult and can be unreliable as changes occurred from time to time and these were often not documented. The date chosen coincides with the start of the car ferry era.

Masters and Mates 1962 | **Engineering Officers 1962**

Vessel	Master	Chief Officer	Second Officer	Chief Engineer	2nd Engineer	3rd Engineer
Lady of Mann	G.R. Kinley	F. Cannell	J.E. Ronan	E.H. Bridson	J.P. Heaton	J. Shields A. Collister
Ben-my-Chree	R. Clucas	T.H. Cubbon	C.H. Collister	W.A. Cain	J. Burden	E. Taylor N. Black
Manx Maid	J.E. Quirk	J.R. Kinley	E.C. Fargher	J.H. Collister	J.W. Craine	R. Motion
Manxman	L. Callow	H.E. Collister	K. Bridson	W.R. Corlett	H. Crawley	R. Kneale A.L. Corkill
Mona's Isle	W.E. McMeiken	M. Maugham	W.Postlethwaite	G. Curphey	R.C. Corkill	L. Corkish B. Johnson
Snaefell	F. Griffin	H.A. Kinley	not known	C. Watterson	T.P. Champion	W.A. Teare T.E. Quilliam
Tynwald	J.D. Craine	J.J. Keig	not known	W.F. Craine	D. Minshall	W.H. Hudson
King Orry	A.W.G. Kissack	W.B. Kinley	not known	A.P. Johnson	W.C. Curphey	G. Mainwaring V. Gilbert
Fenella	T. Corteen	J.S. Kennaugh	J. Costain	A. Costain	J. Steel	D. Pownall
Peveril	H.N. Kinley	J.B. Quirk	W. Cubbon	G.D. Kenna	R.D. Wales	none
Conister	B.C. Corlett	G. Kelly	none	J. Corlett	none	none

The Birth of the Car Ferries

Tenders for the Company's first car ferry, the ***Manx Maid*** went out to seven shipyards, the names of which read like a Who's Who of Britain's best shipbuilders namely: Ailsa Shipbuilding Co Ltd., Troon. Cammell Laird & Co (Shipbuilding & Engineering) Ltd., Birkenhead. Wm Denny & Brothers Ltd., Dumbarton. Harland & Wolff, Belfast. J.I. Thornycroft Ltd., Southampton. Vickers Armstrong Ltd., Barrow-in-Furness and J. Samuel White & Co Ltd., Cowes, Isle of Wight.

Above: The **Manx Maid** *on her sea trials which took place off Arran on 18th and 19th May 1962. (photo: Author's collection)*

Completion of the ***Manx Maid,*** the first Manx ship equipped with anti-roll stabilisers, took place in time for her to run her sea trials on the Clyde on 18th and 19th May 1962. She was powered by steam turbines producing 9,500 s.h.p. and attained a mean speed of 21.69 knots, comfortably above her designed contract speed. Built by Cammell Laird & Co (Shipbuilders and Engineers) Ltd., Yard number 1303 she was launched by Mrs. Joan Alexander wife of Mr. A. Alexander, one of directors of the Steam Packet Company on 23rd January 1962. Being the first of her class, much publicity material was generated including souvenir brochures, newspaper supplements and the like. In common with the other cross channel ships at the time, the ***Manx Maid*** was built to provide separate accommodation for first and second class passengers of which she could carry a total of 1,400.

Above: The maiden voyage of the **Manx Maid** *was from Liverpool on 23rd May 1962. As fate would have it, a strong wind blew up at the crucial moment and the new ship needed the assistance of tugs to get away from the landing stage. As we shall see later in the book, this was far from being the only occasion that assistance from tugs was needed. (photo: Liverpool Daily Post & Echo)*

A selection of early **Manx Maid** *brochures and timetables for 1962. One 1962 brochure is illustrated with an artists impression of the new car ferry* **Manx Maid.** *Note the new motto "Carefree Car-free" The advertised prices to Liverpool were £3.00 for a first class return passenger ticket. Second class cost £2.50. Return fares for vehicles were £6.50 for a Mini, whilst a solo motorcycle could travel for £3.00*
(archive material: Author's collection)

A beautiful period photograph of the Steam Packet warehouse at Douglas in which they garaged their fleet of delivery lorries. Foden, Scammell and Commer trucks are to be seen and it should be noted that horse drawn deliveries, for which the company maintained a stable of 17 horses latterly, were only finally phased out around 1950. (photo: Bill Peters)

Lloyd's Register of Shipping

Lloyds Register of Shipping Certificates of Class. The author holds the original certificates for the ***Manx Maid*** from which these illustrations have been reproduced.

Lloyds Register of Shipping is now well over 200 years old and is the oldest and largest of the world's ship classification societies. From the moment of conception of any vessel which is to be classed, right through the whole design and construction process, Lloyds surveyors are involved at every stage from keel laying to sea trials. Following continuing and painstaking survey and minute examination for durability and reliability the new ship will have earned the accolade ✠100A1. This certificate of quality assurance will enable her to be easily insured and to be totally acceptable to the whole shipping and transport industry for as long as she continues to have the periodic surveys required by Lloyds to remain in class.

The ***Manx Maid*** and the other car ferries were classified **✠100A1 Irish Channel Service** – the highest qualification possible. Ships are built to their owners specification and the requirements are laid down in black and white covering every aspect of the ship's construction and expected performance. Let it suffice to say that the Manx ships were always of the highest standard and to quote from the author's original version of the 120 page specification book for the ***Manx Maid,*** "The workmanship throughout the vessel is to be of the best and highest character and the owners inspectors shall have the power to reject either material or workmanship or both which in their opinion are not reasonably suitable for a first class passenger and mail steamship..."

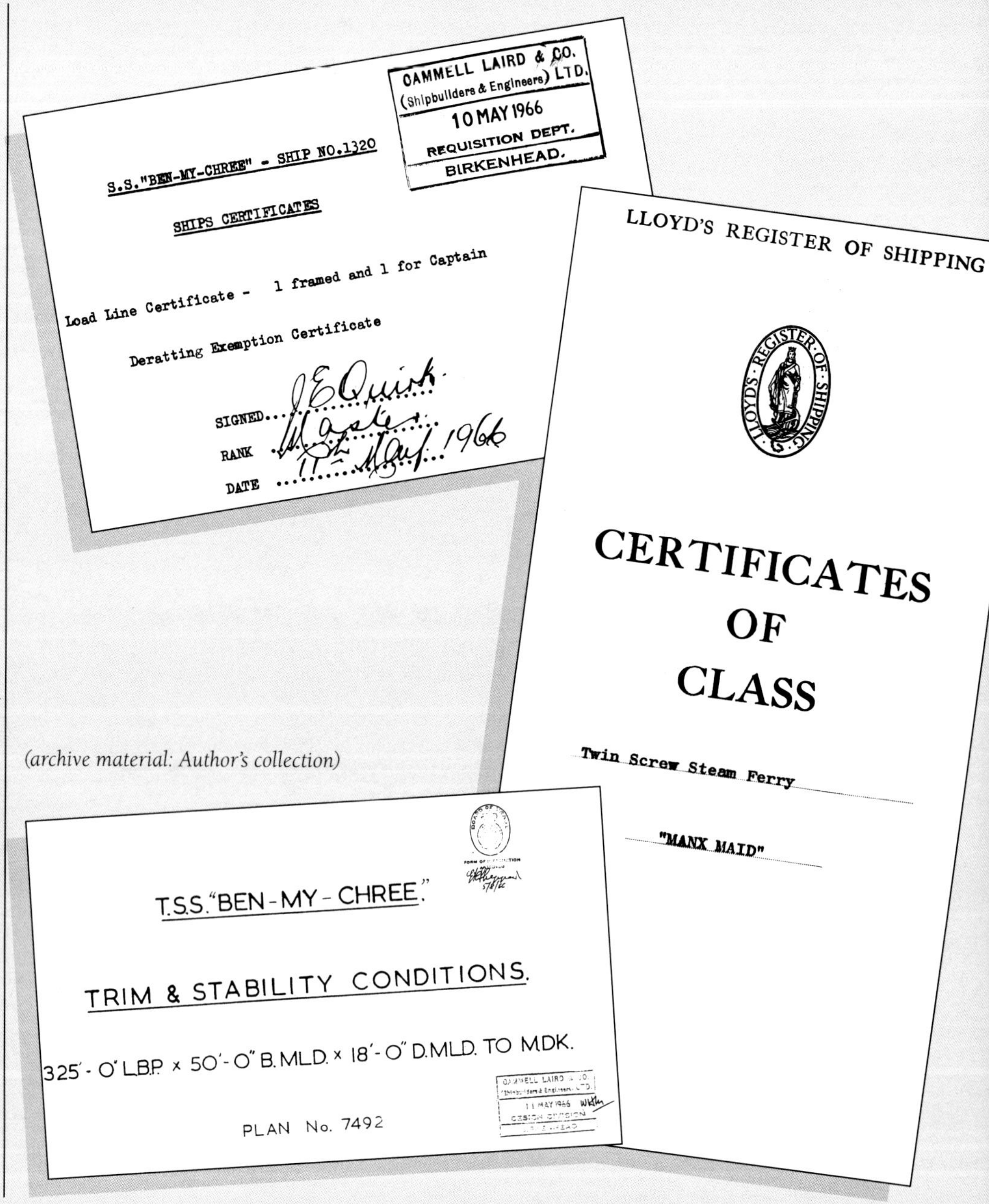

CAMMELL LAIRD & CO. (Shipbuilders & Engineers) LTD.
10 MAY 1966
REQUISITION DEPT.
BIRKENHEAD.

S.S."BEN-MY-CHREE" - SHIP NO.1320

SHIPS CERTIFICATES

Load Line Certificate - 1 framed and 1 for Captain

Deratting Exemption Certificate

SIGNED J E Quirk.
RANK Master.
DATE 11th May 1966

LLOYD'S REGISTER OF SHIPPING

CERTIFICATES OF CLASS

Twin Screw Steam Ferry

"MANX MAID"

T.S.S."BEN-MY-CHREE."

TRIM & STABILITY CONDITIONS.

325'-0" L.B.P. × 50'-0" B.MLD. × 18'-0" D.MLD. TO MDK.

PLAN No. 7492

(archive material: Author's collection)

CERTIFIED. COPY.

Lloyd's Register of Shipping.

Form L.L. 2. (Special.)

FOUNDED 1760. RE-CONSTITUTED 1834.

No. 63876

International Load Line Certificate

Issued under the authority of the Government of the United Kingdom of Great Britain and Northern Ireland under the provisions of the International Load Line Convention, 1930.

Official Number 186352

Ship's Name "MANX MAID"

Port of Registry DOUGLAS

Gross Tonnage 2,726

Freeboard

Load Line.

inches above S.

Tropical feet

Summer

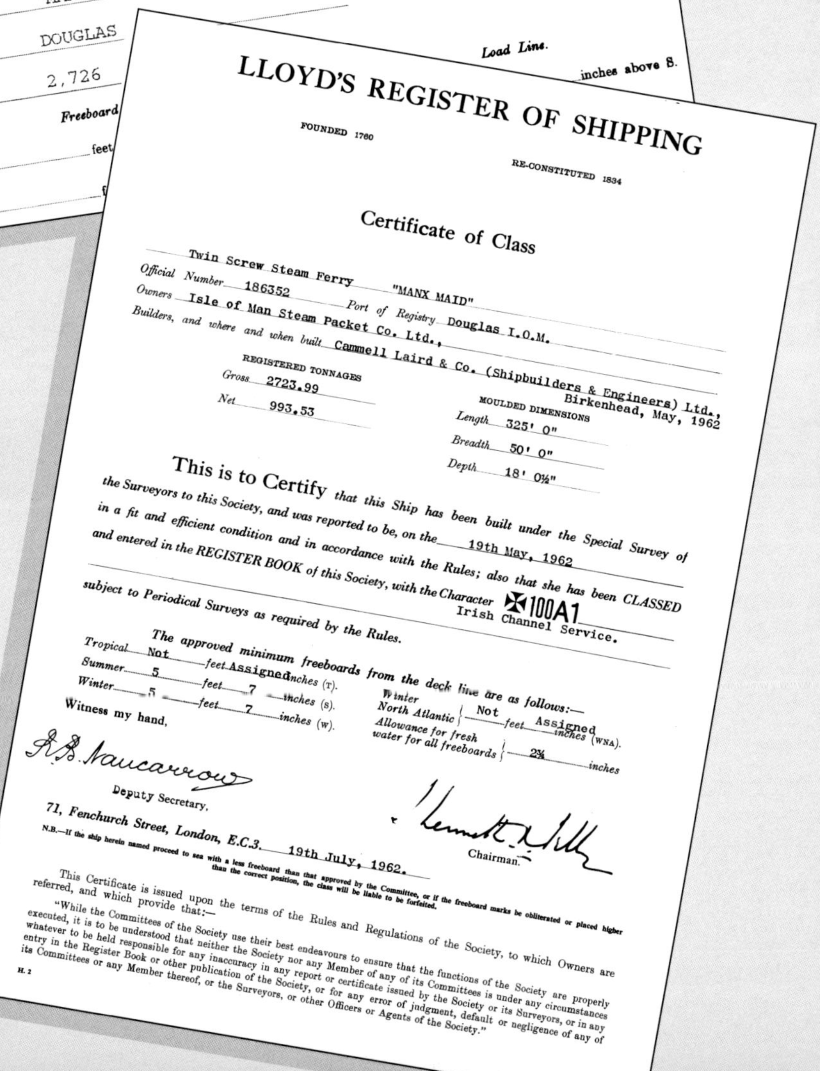

LLOYD'S REGISTER OF SHIPPING

FOUNDED 1760

RE-CONSTITUTED 1834

Certificate of Class

Twin Screw Steam Ferry "MANX MAID"

Official Number 186352 *Port of Registry* Douglas I.O.M.

Owners Isle of Man Steam Packet Co. Ltd.,

Builders, and where and when built Cammell Laird & Co. (Shipbuilders & Engineers) Ltd., Birkenhead, May, 1962

REGISTERED TONNAGES

Gross 2723.99

Net 993.53

MOULDED DIMENSIONS

Length 325' 0"

Breadth 50' 0"

Depth 18' 0½"

This is to Certify *that this Ship has been built under the Special Survey of the Surveyors to this Society, and was reported to be, on the* 19th May, 1962 *in a fit and efficient condition and in accordance with the Rules; also that she has been CLASSED and entered in the REGISTER BOOK of this Society, with the Character* ✠100A1 Irish Channel Service.

subject to Periodical Surveys as required by the Rules.

The approved minimum freeboards from the deck line are as follows:—

Tropical Not *feet* Assigned *inches* (T).

Summer 5 *feet* 7 *inches* (S).

Winter 5 *feet* 7 *inches* (W).

Winter North Atlantic Not *feet* Assigned *inches* (WNA).

Allowance for fresh water for all freeboards 2⅝ *inches*

Witness my hand,

Deputy Secretary,

Chairman.

71, Fenchurch Street, London, E.C.3. 19th July, 1962.

N.B.—If the ship herein named proceed to sea with a less freeboard than that approved by the Committee, or if the freeboard marks be obliterated or placed higher than the correct position, the class will be liable to be forfeited.

This Certificate is issued upon the terms of the Rules and Regulations of the Society, to which Owners are referred, and which provide that:—

"While the Committees of the Society use their best endeavours to ensure that the functions of the Society are properly executed, it is to be understood that neither the Society nor any Member of any of its Committees is under any circumstances whatever to be held responsible for any inaccuracy in any report or certificate issued by the Society or its Surveyors, or in any entry in the Register Book or other publication of the Society, or for any error of judgment, default or negligence of any of its Committees or any Member thereof, or the Surveyors, or other Officers or Agents of the Society."

H. 2

It is important to know how any ship is likely to behave under different operational conditions, however extreme they may be. Therefore before a passenger ship enters service and from time to time throughout its service life, its centre of gravity is ascertained experimentally by inclining the ship with weights on deck and her stability is calculated for at least eight different states of loading.

These represent all the conditions that the master of the ship is likely to encounter with regard to the total payload, passengers, number of vehicles aboard, weight of any cargo, amount of fuel and water (more at the beginning of the voyage than at the end) ballast etc. From this he understands how his ship will behave under different conditions and trim and what are her safe limits of operation. *Will she be tender, cranky or stiff?* These are by far the most important calculations affecting the safety of the ship and are done to enable her to survive even the most extreme events. In the ultimate disaster, the ship is designed to protect her human cargo by staying afloat as long as possible but if she cannot survive, in the end she is designed to sink slowly, upright and in a controlled way so that lifeboats can be launched and passengers thereby saved. The original Trim and Stability Conditions Books in which are recorded the calculations for both the ***Manx Maid*** and the ***Ben-my-Chree*** survive in the author's possession along with much other vital information. Both stipulated that in the worst permitted stability condition with bunkers and tanks empty and the ships' centre of gravity high, "the carriage of vehicles above the lowest half landing is only permitted in fair weather". It should not come as any surprise for readers to see that tremendous care is taken to ensure the absolute safety of passengers aboard the ships of the Isle of Man Steam Packet Company.

The Arrival of the Manx Maid

The imminent arrival of the **Manx Maid** and the closure of the Fleetwood berth at the end of the 1961 season rendered one passenger ship virtually redundant and it was decided to sell the 1946 built ***Mona's Queen***. Several interested parties visited the ship and also the ***King Orry.*** In the end in October 1962, the ***Mona's Queen*** she was sold to a Chandris subsidiary named Marvic Navigation Inc. for further service in the Mediterranean.

The arrival of the **Manx Maid** *for the first time at Douglas was regarded as a matter of national importance. Large crowds gathered at every vantage point especially on the Victoria Pier where the ship was to berth. It is interesting to note how harbour security has changed over the years since May 1962 and that these days during passenger ship movements, the piers are strictly out of bounds except for travelling passengers. Expert commercial photographer, Bill Peters (Manx Press Pictures) took these photographs and he had his shop and processing works next to Mrs Berry's sweet shop in Prospect Hill, Douglas (roughly where Victory House new wing now stands). He was always very friendly towards the author and was willing to offer tips on photographic technique too.*

(photos: Bill Peters)

An early classic photograph of the **Manx Maid** *at her berth on the south side of the King Edward Pier. Reminiscent of John Masefield's famous poem "Cargoes", her funnel is salt-caked and some of the colour has bleached out indicative of a hard winters work, probably one of her first.*
(photo: Author's collection)

On 22nd August 1963, transport photographer Norman Jones took these two excellent photographs aboard the **Manx Maid.** *They show Chief Officer (later captain and fleet commodore) J.S. (John) Kennaugh attending to the stabiliser controls and 2nd Officer (later captain) Ken Bridson working the radio direction finding equipment.*

(photos: Norman Jones)

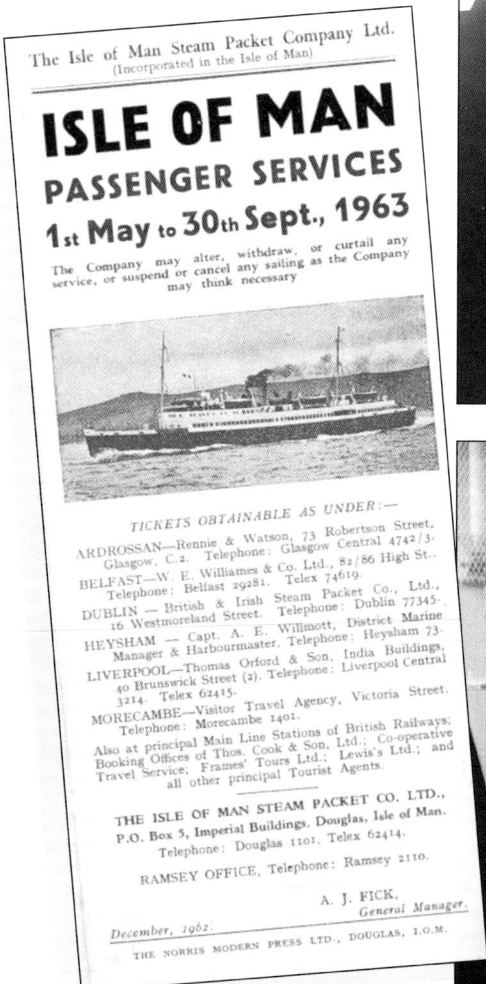

The Isle of Man Steam Packet Company Ltd.
(Incorporated in the Isle of Man)

ISLE OF MAN

PASSENGER SERVICES

1st May to 30th Sept., 1963

The Company may alter, withdraw, or curtail any service, or suspend or cancel any sailing as the Company may think necessary

TICKETS OBTAINABLE AS UNDER:—

ARDROSSAN—Rennie & Watson, 73 Robertson Street, Glasgow, C.2. Telephone: Glasgow Central 4742/3.

BELFAST—W. E. Williames & Co. Ltd., 82/86 High St., Telephone: Belfast 29281. Telex 74619.

DUBLIN — British & Irish Steam Packet Co., Ltd., 16 Westmoreland Street. Telephone: Dublin 77345.

HEYSHAM — Capt. A. E. Willmott, District Marine Manager & Harbourmaster. Telephone: Heysham 73.

LIVERPOOL—Thomas Orford & Son, India Buildings, 40 Brunswick Street (2). Telephone: Liverpool Central 3214. Telex 62415.

MORECAMBE—Visitor Travel Agency, Victoria Street. Telephone: Morecambe 1401.

Also at principal Main Line Stations of British Railways; Booking Offices of Thos. Cook & Son, Ltd.; Co-operative Travel Service; Frames' Tours Ltd.; Lewis's Ltd.; and all other principal Tourist Agents.

THE ISLE OF MAN STEAM PACKET CO. LTD., P.O. Box 5, Imperial Buildings, Douglas, Isle of Man.
Telephone: Douglas 1101. Telex 62414.

RAMSEY OFFICE, Telephone: Ramsey 2110.

A. J. FICK,
General Manager.

December, 1962.

THE NORRIS MODERN PRESS LTD., DOUGLAS, I.O.M.

1963 timetable.

(archive material: Author's collection)

In 1963 a document of national importance was published by H.M.S.O. entitled "The reshaping of British Railways". It quickly became known simply as "The Beeching Report" and its swingeing measures were referred to as the falling of Dr. Beeching's Axe. As with trains, railway shipping services were also to suffer greatly and many of the routes thereby closed were re-opened, or similar ones established, by rivals who could hardly believe their good fortune. One such operator was Otto Thoresen from Norway who stepped in at Southampton with vessels that were to set the benchmark standard for years to come.

In 1964 the new Thoresen Car Ferries ship **Viking II** *was on a round Britain promotional trip to introduce her to the travel trade and public. This superb, atmospheric photograph of the* **Manx Maid,** *taking on bunkers from the oiling barge* **Perso** *was taken by the author's good friend Ray Pugh who was aboard the* **Viking II** *at the Liverpool Landing stage when 10,000 people are reported to have visited the ship on 27th and 28th October.*

(photo: Ray Pugh)

The Ben-my-Chree

The ***Ben-my-Chree*** (Manx Gaelic for "girl of my heart") was the Steam Packet Company's second car ferry and having been ordered in April 1964 she was built as yard number 1320 by Cammell Lairds' just as had been her older sister, the ***Manx Maid.***

She was very similar to the ***Manx Maid*** but had slightly different arrangements at the forward end of the promenade deck especially in the area beneath the wheelhouse. The wheelhouse window arrangements were also different as were those on the shelter deck and the staging for the liferafts on the ***Ben-my-Chree*** on the boat deck was far higher than on the earlier ship. When built she did not have the traditional triple chime steam organ pipe whistle set but had a steam powered siren which made an altogether less pleasant, almost rasping single note. These were the obvious differences that enabled identification at first glance but there were plenty of others, less obvious. Her stabilisers were to be effective down to speeds of only 14 knots whilst those of the ***Manx Maid*** really only worked properly at full speed. All in all, she was a very superior ship and one that carried the author and his family on many voyages in storms and calm weather throughout her all too short, nineteen year career.

The **Ben-my-Chree** *was launched by Mrs. Margaret Brownsdon wife of Major T.E. Brownsdon one of the directors, later Chairman, on 10th December 1965.*

(photo: Author's collection)

The construction progress of the new car ferry ***Ben-my-Chree*** enabled the ageing passenger ship dating from 1927 of the same name (with the suffix II added to free the name for the new ship) to be withdrawn and offered for sale for scrap. Her boilers had been giving considerable trouble and would shortly need replacing or major surgery if she was to remain operational. She was sold to Van Heyghen Freres, Ghent, Belgium at the end of November 1965 and was towed away that December to be scrapped.

Above: The **Ben-my-Chree** *(1927) at Liverpool. (photo: Ray Pugh)*

Right: Brochures for October to December 1966 and January to April 1967.
The **Ben-my-Chree** *was the last passenger ship built for the Company with accommodation separated into first and second classes, she was their last steam powered ship and the last to be built at Cammell Lairds' for the Steam Packet Company.*
The final prices for two class travel up to 31st December 1966 were as follows:
First Class return £3.50 Second Class return £3.00
From 1st January 1967 the return fare became £3.42 , rather more than splitting the difference between the old first and second class fares. On the same date a special two day ticket offering return travel for a single fare was available at £2.00.
(archive material: Author's collection)

The **Ben-my-Chree** *ran her sea trials on the Skelmorlie Mile, near the Isle of Arran on the Clyde on 10th May 1966.* *(photo: Author's Collection)*

Here we see the **Manx Maid** *early in her career, enjoying a heave off the Princes Landing Stage at Liverpool by the Alexander tug* **Huskisson.**
(photo: Ray Pugh)

When built, neither the ***Manx Maid*** nor the ***Ben-my-Chree*** had bow side thrust units. Until 1978 (***Ben-my-Chree***) and 1979 (***Manx Maid***) when they finally had bow thrusters fitted and operating, both car ferries had to resort to a helping tow from tugs when strong winds pinned them to the berth. Their bow thrust units were very unusual in that they were steam powered, turbine driven propeller sets, taking main steam straight from the ship's boilers along a heavily lagged steam pipe running the length of the vehicle deck-head. On the later car ferries ***Mona's Queen*** and ***Lady of Mann***, bow thrusters were powered by 500 h.p. electric motors.

Below: Nowhere was there to be found the famous "brotherhood of the sea" bonding more strongly than amongst the masters and other officers of the Steam Packet Company. Here we see an exchange of "Marconigrams" between Captain A.W.G. (Westby) Kissack (later marine superintendent) of the **Manx Maid** *and Captain T.H. (Tom) Corteen who was taking the fabled* **Lady of Mann** *(1930) away to Barrow-in-Furness on 17th August 1971 to await her fate.*

(archive material: Capt. Westby Kissack)

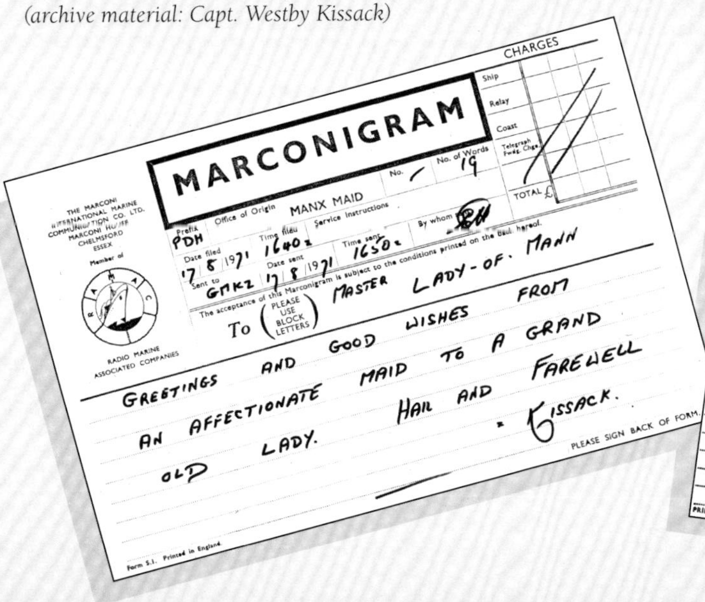
THE MARCONI INTERNATIONAL MARINE COMMUNICATION CO. LTD. MARCONI HOUSE CHELMSFORD ESSEX

Member of R A M A C

RADIO MARINE ASSOCIATED COMPANIES

MARCONIGRAM

CHARGES: Ship / Relay / Coast / Telegraph Fwdg. Chge. / TOTAL £

No. 1 — No. of Words 19

Prefix PDH — Office of Origin MANX MAID — Service Instructions

Time filed 1640z — By whom

Date filed 17 8 1971 — Date sent 17 8 1971 — Time sent 1650z

Sent to GMKZ

The acceptance of this Marconigram is subject to the conditions printed on the back hereof.

To (PLEASE USE BLOCK LETTERS) MASTER LADY-OF-MANN

GREETINGS AND GOOD WISHES FROM AN AFFECTIONATE MAID TO A GRAND OLD LADY. HAIL AND FAREWELL = KISSACK.

PLEASE SIGN BACK OF FORM.

Form S.1. Printed in England

S-3 THE MARCONI INTERNATIONAL MARINE CO. LTD. ELETTRA HOUSE CHELMSFORD ESSEX

MARCONI MARINE

MARCONIGRAM

Prefix PDH — Handed in at LADY OF MANN — No. 1 — No. of Words 26 — Date 17.8.71 — Time 1725 — Service Instructions

Date Received 17.8.71 — Time Received 1735z — Received from GMKZ — By

TO MASTER MANX MAID

THE OLD LADY THANKS THE YOUNG MAID FOR HER AFFECTIONATE GREETINGS AND HOPES THAT SHE TOO WILL GROW INTO A GRAND OLD MAID = CORTEEN.

PRINTED IN ENGLAND

PTO

This photograph from Captain W.E. McMeiken's collection shows both the steam car ferries **Manx Maid** *and* **Ben-my-Chree** *laid up at Barrow during the 1966 seamens strike. Captain McMeiken was master of the* **Manx Maid** *and Captain J.E. Quirk (commodore) was in the new* **Ben-my-Chree.** *The rest of the fleet was mostly at Birkenhead except the* **Peveril** *which was at Coburg Dock on the Liverpool side, the* **Lady of Mann** *was at Langton dry-dock before crossing to Birkenhead, the* **Fenella** *was in the inner harbour at Douglas and the* **Ramsey** *was in the inner harbour of her own namesake port. (photo: Capt. W.E. McMeiken collection)*

Summer 1970 sees the **Ben-my-Chree** *arriving at Douglas with a good load of passengers in evidence. (photo: George Danielson)*

The ***Ben-my-Chree*** operated her maiden voyage on 12th May 1966 and an inaugural cruise round the Island on 15th May. Both the ***Ben-my-Chree*** and the ***Manx Maid*** sailed to Liverpool that evening and thence to Barrow to lay-up for the duration of the seamens' strike.

When the strike was over, the ***Manx Maid*** opened the first car ferry service to Ardrossan sailing from Douglas shortly before midnight on 2nd July and returning from Ardrossan at 12 noon on 3rd July 1966.

The T.T. races which had been postponed for two months, were run belatedly.

THE ISLE OF MAN STEAM PACKET COMPANY LIMITED
(Incorporated in the Isle of Man)

WELCOME RETURN OF THE
FLEETWOOD
TO DOUGLAS
STEAMER SERVICE

Enjoy a . . .
DAY EXCURSION
on
WEDNESDAY . 25th AUGUST
THURSDAY . . 26th AUGUST
FRIDAY . . . . . 27th AUGUST
SUNDAY . . . . 29th AUGUST
MONDAY . . . . . . 30th AUGUST
TUESDAY . . . . . . 31st AUGUST
WEDNESDAY . 1st SEPTEMBER
THURSDAY . . 2nd SEPTEMBER
also
SUNDAY 12th, MONDAY 13th and TUESDAY 14th SEPTEMBE

FLEETWOOD
Depart 10-30 a.m.
DOUGLAS
Depart 5-0 p.m.
Allowing about 3½ hours ashore in Douglas

DAY RETURN FARE £2
Children 3 and under 14 years Half-fare
Tickets obtainable from Booking Office alongside Steamer on day o

Passengers travelling to the Isle of Man on holiday can use the services. The return
the inward and outward journeys are made on Tuesday, Wednesday or Thursday, in
£4.70. Return portions of Fleetwood tickets are valid for return to Liverpool without ext
No motor vehicles can be conveyed. Any enquiries regarding the services should b
Office of the Company.

For 1972 the Company intends to open the service about end of MAY and contin
frequency will be decided and published by the year-end, but will be mid-week
Sundays during the high season.

All steamers are fully licensed and there are buffets for light refreshments.

The Company may alter, withdraw or curtail any service or suspend or cancel
may think necessary.

PASSENGERS AND THEIR ACCOMPANIED LUGGAGE will only be carried subj
Conditions of Carriage of Passengers and Passengers' Accompanied Property
Offices and on board its vessels. Acceptance of a ticket issued by the Compa
conditions.

IMPERIAL BUILDINGS, DOUGLAS.
Telephone 0624 3824

B. & Hx. Ltd., I.O.M.

1971 handbill announcing the return of sailings to Fleetwood. British Transport Docks announced in 1959 that the state of the old wooden wharf at Fleetwood was giving serious grounds for concern and that they could not guarantee it would be safe to use in 1960. Sailings actually ceased the following year on 11th September 1961 due to the poor condition of the wharf and finally they were resumed on 25th August 1971 after it had been rebuilt in concrete. (archive material: Author's collection)

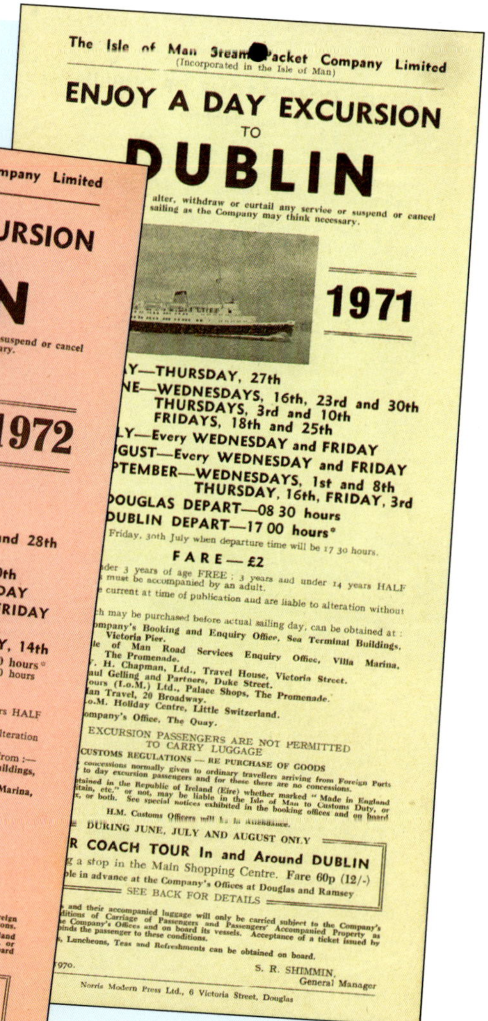

The Isle of Man Steam Packet Company Limited
(Incorporated in the Isle of Man)

ENJOY A DAY EXCURSION
TO
DUBLIN
alter, withdraw or curtail any service or suspend or cancel
sailing as the Company may think necessary.

1971

Y—THURSDAY, 27th
NE—WEDNESDAYS, 16th, 23rd and 30th
THURSDAYS, 3rd and 10th
FRIDAYS, 18th and 25th
LY—Every WEDNESDAY and FRIDAY
GUST—Every WEDNESDAY and FRIDAY
PTEMBER—WEDNESDAYS, 1st and 8th
THURSDAY, 16th, FRIDAY, 3rd
DOUGLAS DEPART—08 30 hours
DUBLIN DEPART—17 00 hours*
Friday, 30th July when departure time will be 17 30 hours.

FARE—£2

der 3 years of age FREE; 3 years and under 14 years HALF
must be accompanied by an adult.
current at time of publication and are liable to alteration without

h may be purchased before actual sailing day, can be obtained at:
mpany's Booking and Enquiry Office, Sea Terminal Buildings,
Victoria Pier.
le of Man Road Services Enquiry Office, Villa Marina,
The Promenade.
. H. Chapman, Ltd., Travel House, Victoria Street.
aul Gelling and Partners, Duke Street.
ours (I.o.M.) Ltd., Palace Shops, The Promenade.
an Travel, 20 Broadway.
.o.M. Holiday Centre, Little Switzerland.
mpany's Office, The Quay.

EXCURSION PASSENGERS ARE NOT PERMITTED
TO CARRY LUGGAGE

CUSTOMS REGULATIONS — RE PURCHASE OF GOODS
concessions normally given to ordinary travellers arriving from Foreign Ports
to day excursion passengers and for these there are no concessions.
tained in the Republic of Ireland (Eire) whether marked "Made in England
itain, etc." or not, may be liable in the Isle of Man to Customs Duty, or
, or both. See special notices exhibited in the booking offices and on board

H.M. Customs Officers will be in attendance.

DURING JUNE, JULY AND AUGUST ONLY
R COACH TOUR In and Around DUBLIN
g a stop in the Main Shopping Centre. Fare 60p (12/-)
le in advance at the Company's Offices at Douglas and Ramsey
SEE BACK FOR DETAILS

and their accompanied luggage will only be carried subject to the Company's
ditions of Carriage of Passengers and Passengers' Accompanied Property as
e Company's Offices and on board its vessels. Acceptance of a ticket issued by
binds the passenger to these conditions.
, Luncheons, Teas and Refreshments can be obtained on board.

1970.

S. R. SHIMMIN,
General Manager

Norris Modern Press Ltd., 6 Victoria Street, Douglas

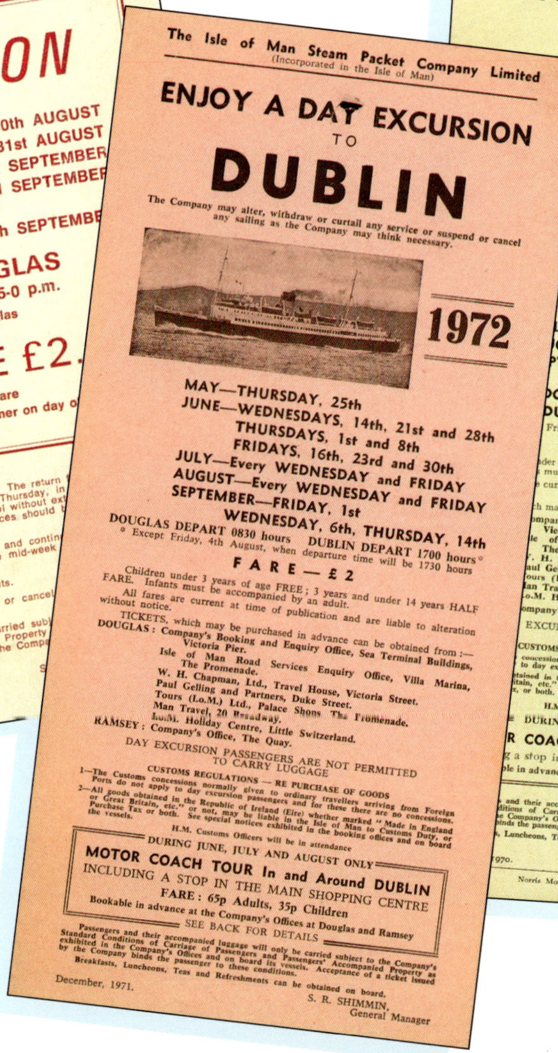

The Isle of Man Steam Packet Company Limited
(Incorporated in the Isle of Man)

ENJOY A DAY EXCURSION
TO
DUBLIN
The Company may alter, withdraw or curtail any service or suspend or cancel any sailing as the Company may think necessary.

1972

MAY—THURSDAY, 25th
JUNE—WEDNESDAYS, 14th, 21st and 28th
THURSDAYS, 1st and 8th
FRIDAYS, 16th, 23rd and 30th
JULY—Every WEDNESDAY and FRIDAY
AUGUST—Every WEDNESDAY and FRIDAY
SEPTEMBER—FRIDAY, 1st
WEDNESDAY, 6th, THURSDAY, 14th
DOUGLAS DEPART 0830 hours DUBLIN DEPART 1700 hours*
* Except Friday, 4th August, when departure time will be 1730 hours

FARE — £2

Children under 3 years of age FREE; 3 years and under 14 years HALF FARE. Infants must be accompanied by an adult.

All fares are current at time of publication and are liable to alteration without notice.

TICKETS, which may be purchased in advance can be obtained from:—
DOUGLAS: Company's Booking and Enquiry Office, Sea Terminal Buildings, Victoria Pier.
Isle of Man Road Services Enquiry Office, Villa Marina, The Promenade.
W. H. Chapman, Ltd., Travel House, Victoria Street.
Paul Gelling and Partners, Duke Street.
Tours (I.o.M.) Ltd., Palace Shops, The Promenade.
Man Travel, 20 Broadway.
I.o.M. Holiday Centre, Little Switzerland.
RAMSEY: Company's Office, The Quay.

DAY EXCURSION PASSENGERS ARE NOT PERMITTED TO CARRY LUGGAGE

CUSTOMS REGULATIONS — RE PURCHASE OF GOODS
1—The Customs concessions normally given to ordinary travellers arriving from Foreign Ports do not apply to day excursion passengers and for these there are no concessions.
2—All goods obtained in the Republic of Ireland (Eire) whether marked "Made in England or Great Britain, etc." or not, may be liable in the Isle of Man to Customs Duty, or Purchase Tax or both. See special notices exhibited in the booking offices and on board the vessels.

H.M. Customs Officers will be in attendance

DURING JUNE, JULY AND AUGUST ONLY
MOTOR COACH TOUR In and Around DUBLIN
INCLUDING A STOP IN THE MAIN SHOPPING CENTRE
FARE: 65p Adults, 35p Children
Bookable in advance at the Company's Offices at Douglas and Ramsey
SEE BACK FOR DETAILS

Passengers and their accompanied luggage will only be carried subject to the Company's Standard Conditions of Carriage of Passengers and Passengers' Accompanied Property as exhibited in the Company's Offices and on board its vessels. Acceptance of a ticket issued by the Company binds the passenger to these conditions.
Breakfasts, Luncheons, Teas and Refreshments can be obtained on board.

December, 1971.

S. R. SHIMMIN,
General Manager

1971 and 1972 handbills announcing excursions to Dublin. It is interesting to see that on the 1971 handbill, the vessel illustrated is the **Ben-my-Chree** *yet there was to be no car ferry service to Dublin until 1974. By 1972 the Company had realised the error of its ways and the handbill featured the passenger steamer* **Manxman**. *(archive material: Author's collection)*

Captain W.E. (Ernie) McMeiken retired in March 1972 and Captain Kissack became commodore in his place. This interesting line up of Steam Packet masters attending the retirement presentation is as follows (left to right). Captains Lyndhurst Callow, Westby Kissack, George Kinley, Ernie McMeiken, Frank Griffin (marine superintendent), Walter Cubbon and Eddie Quirk. *(archive material: Capt. Westby Kissack)*

The need for a third car ferry was finally determined by the deteriorating condition of the famous old ***Lady of Mann*** (1930). Her Lloyds Load Line certificate was due to expire in June 1972 and clearly she was in no condition to come through survey without a lot of money being spent on her to meet current regulations. Her passenger certificate had been reduced as had her operating range. In the event in December 1969, Ailsa Shipbuilding Co. Ltd. produced the successful tender for the new ship to be delivered in the Spring of 1972.

The **Lady of Mann** *(1930)* *(photo: Author's collection)*

The Mona's Queen

The name ***Mona's Queen*** was chosen and given to the ship on 21st December 1971 by Mrs. Daphne Cowley, wife of Mr. Ken Cowley a director. However, she was not actually launched until the next day in a ceremony that was delayed for twenty-four hours on account of gales. The ***Mona's Queen*** was launched with her main diesel engines fully installed but even then it was considered she would be too light in the water to launch safely in gale force winds.

In these three photographs we see the ship on the slipway awaiting her delayed launch, and then going "down the ways" and finally fully afloat and having loose baulks of timber and other shipyard debris removed following the successful launch.
(photos: Capt. Westby Kissack collection)

Left: The fitting out of the **Mona's Queen** *fell behind schedule not only on account of shipyard strikes but also the infamous three day week invoked at the time of the 1972 mine workers strikes under the British Government's emergency powers. Problems continued and sea trails were delayed on several occasions. Vibrations from the ship's diesel engines, the Steam Packet Company's first installation of diesels in one of its passenger ships, and oscillation causing gearbox problems and leaking stern shafts were the cause of great concern. In the end she ran sea trials on 4th June 1972 when she achieved 21.21 knots and was handed over four days later. The photograph is of the* **Mona's Queen** *running her sea trials.*
(photo: Author's collection)

Below: Sailing arrangements for the week 2nd to 8th June 1972 showing Captain Kissack's hand-written update for his new ship's inaugural sailings.
(archive material: Capt. Westby Kissack)

PRIVATE AND NOT FOR CIRCULATION

VICTORIA PRESS LTD.

THE ISLE OF MAN STEAM PACKET COMPANY LIMITED.

Sailing Arrangements—Friday, 2nd June to Thursday, 8th June, 1972.

SUBJECT TO ALTERATION WITHOUT NOTICE

B.S.T.	FRIDAY, 2nd JUNE	SATURDAY, 3rd Production Race 750 c.c. Sidecar	SUNDAY, 4th	MONDAY, 5th Junior Race 500 c.c. Sidecar	TUESDAY, 6th	WEDNESDAY, 7th 250 c.c. Lightweight 750 c.c. Formula	THURSDAY, 8th
High Water at Douglas	02.52 16.2 15.19 14.5	03.39 15.7 16.09 14.1	04.29 15.3 17.06 13.7	05.29 15.0 18.09 13.7	06.33 15.0 19.16 14.1	07.40 15.4 20.22 15.0	08.46 16.2 21.24 16.1
MONA'S QUEEN A.W.G. Kissack						TROON to D'glas 1900	arr DO 0115. D–L 2300
BEN-MY-CHREE ... ... Capt. H. N. Kinley	D. to L. 09.00 L. to D. 15.30—2nd. D. to L.—p.m.	L. to D. 01.00—3rd. D. to L.—a.m. L. to D. 11.00—2nd. D. to L. 16.00—2nd.	L. to D. 01.00 D. to L. 09.30—2nd. L. to D. 16.00—2nd.	D. to L. 18.00	L. to D. 10.30 D. to L. 16.00	L. to D. 10.30 D. to L. 18.00	L. to D. 10.30 D. to L. 16.00—2nd.
MANX MAID ... ... Capt. Kennaugh	L. to D. 08.00 D. to L.—p.m. L. to D. 18.00—1st. 3/4 D. to L.—p.m.	L. to D. 01.00—5th. D. to L. 09.00—3rd. L. to D. 15.30—3rd. 1/4 ~~D. [illegible] 2355~~	~~D. to Ardrossan—a.m.~~ Ardrossan to D. 12.00 1½	D. to L. 09.00 L. to D. 15.30 1/4	D. to L. 09.00 L. to D. 15.30 1/4	D. to L. 09.00 L. to D. 15.30 1/4	D. to L. 09.00—2nd. L. to D. 15.30 1/2 D. to L.—p.m.
MANXMAN ... ... Capt. J R. Kinley	L. to D. 10.30—1st. D. to L. 14.30 L. to D. 18.00—2nd.	D. to L.—a.m. L. to D. 10.00—2nd. D. to L. 16.00—1st.	L. to D. 16.00—1st.	PD	D to Llandudno—a.m. Llandudno to D. 10.15 D. to Belfast—p.m.	Young Farmers Charter Belfast to D. 07.30 D. to Belfast 18.45.	Belfast to D.—a.m. D. to L. 16.00—1st.
MONA'S ISLE ... ... Capt. Quirk	D. to L.—a.m. L. to D. 10.30—2nd. D. to L. 16.00	L. to D. 01.00—1st. D. to L.—a.m. L. to D. 11.00—1st. D. to L. 23.55	L. to Llandudno 11.15 Cruise 14.30 Llandudno to L. 17.15	L. to D. 10.30	D. to Llandudno 17.30 PD 1400	Llandudno to D. 10.15	D. to Dublin 08.30 Dublin to D. 17.00
SNAEFELL ... ... Capt. Collister	D. to L.—a.m. 3/4 L. to D. 10.30—3rd. D. to L.—p.m. 3/4	L. to D. 01.00—2nd. 1 D. to L. 09.00—1st. L. to D. 15.30—1st. 3/4	D. to L. 09.30—1st.	L. to D. 01.00 1/4 D. to L. 16.00 1/2		L. to D. 01.00 3/4 D. to Llandudno 17.30 Llandudno to D.—p.m. 3/4	D. to L. 09.00—1st.
TYNWALD ... ... Capt. Ronan	D. to Belfast 09.00 Belfast to D. 17.00 D. to L. 23.55	L. to D. 10.00—1st. D. to Ardrossan 15.00	Ardrossan to Dublin—a.m.	**Dublin to D. 08.30** **D. to Dublin 19.30**	Dublin to D.—a.m. 1400 → PD noon	D. to Fleetwood 17.30 Fleetwood to D.—p.m. PD 1400	D. to Belfast 09.00 Belfast to D. 17.00
KING ORRY ... ... Capt. Fargher	D. to L.—a.m. L. to D. 15.30—1st. D. to L.—p.m.	L. to D. 01.00—4th D. to L. 09.00—2nd. L. to D. 15.30—2nd.	PD.	D. to Fleetwood—p.m.	Fleetwood to D. 10.30 D. to Fleetwood 17.30	Fleetwood to D. 10.30 D. to L. 16.00	L. to Llandudno 10.45 Cruise 14.30 Llandudno to L. 17.15
PEVERIL ... ... Capt. Maughan	L. to D. 23.55			D. to L. 18.00		L. to D. 20.00	
FENELLA ... ... Capt. Moore	D. to L. 17.00			L. to D. 18.00		D. to L. 20.00	
RAMSEY ... ... Capt. Bridson			L. to D. 17.00		D. to L. 19.00	L. to D. 20.00	
Wind and Weather							

Sadly the ***Mona's Queen*** had arrived too late for the inward bound lucrative T.T. traffic and her non-availability caused inconvenience to pre-booked vehicular traffic although the needs of passengers were able to be accommodated by the rest of the fleet. Nevertheless, she was able to help with the return traffic. She arrived at Douglas from the builders yard at Troon at 01.15 on 8th June and sailed again at 23.00 to Liverpool ready to take her maiden voyage the next morning at 10.30.

Above: Ailsa Shipbuilding Co. Limited promotional brochure.

Right: 1972 Timetable. (archive material: Author's collection)

On 15th June, just six days into her commercial life whilst on passage from Douglas to Liverpool, the ***Mona's Queen*** sprang an oil leak in her starboard propeller system and she limped on to Liverpool, where with the aid of tugs she arrived and retired to Gladstone dock for new oil seals to be fitted.

The new ship, being wider in the beam by two feet (600 mm) was able to be adapted to carry 200 more passengers than the two older steam powered car ferries. She also required larger stabilisers on account of her greater breadth and lighter draft.

The ***Mona's Queen*** was licensed to carry 1,600 passengers.

On 4th July 1972 the **Mona's Queen** opened the Belfast car ferry service followed by the ***Manx Maid*** a week later. The Company hoped to start Dublin car ferry service the next year but in fact it did not start until 1974.

*Above: The **Mona's Queen's** maiden voyage was finally delayed a further day and was run on 9th June 1972 although planned for the previous day. Here we see the souvenir menu which has been autographed by many directors, managers, captains and their wives.*
(archive material: Capt. Westby Kissack)

Right: Ailsa Shipbuilding presented the Steam Packet Company with a fine painting of the new ship and in this photograph we see it being handed over. Captain Corteen is on the extreme left, Captain McMeiken (left) and Captain Kissack (right) are holding the painting. Steam Packet managers Mr. R. A.(Ronnie) Kissack and Mr. S.R.(Syd) Shimmin look on with Mr. Keith Rae a Steam Packet director, one of the gentlemen on the right.
(archive material: Capt. Westby Kissack)

Llandudno

Top:
Aboard the **St. Trillo.**
(photo: Author)

Until 1962, the sailings from Liverpool to Llandudno, Llandudno to Douglas and short cruises from North Wales ports had been provided by the ships of the Liverpool & North Wales Steamship Company which then finally went into liquidation. After their demise the lively little ***St. Trillo,*** was acquired from the liquidators by the Bristol company P. & A. Campbell Ltd. and until 1969, was operated by them on short trips from Llandudno and Menai Bridge. From 1963 the Steam Packet Company took over the principal sailings.
The possibility of the Isle of Man Steam Packet Company acquiring the ***St. Trillo*** was considered but the idea was quickly discounted as by then she was getting old and unreliable and there was a general paucity of business anyway. Nevertheless, the thought of that diminuative 314 ton ship, with her two funnels in Steam Packet red and black livery, is one that the author still likes to dwell upon! Later, there followed detailed consideration by Mersey Ferries that they too might take over the service but no progress was made in this direction either. In the end, until 1982 (except in 1967 when Llandudno Pier was closed) the Steam Packet Company provided all the sailings to and from North Wales including afternoon cruises from Llandudno (but none from Menai Bridge).

On Sunday 2nd September 1973 the **Ben-my-Chree** *was rostered to sail from Liverpool to Llandudno and onwards for the afternoon cruise along the coast off Anglesey prior to return to Llandudno and later Liverpool. At least until now, this is the only occasion that a Steam Packet Company car ferry has been to Llandudno. These excellent and historic photographs were taken by Ray Pugh and show the* **Ben-my-Chree** *coming alongside, and departing for the afternoon cruise.* *(photos: Ray Pugh)*

(archive material: Author's collection)

SAILINGS FROM LLANDUDNO

(Weather and circumstances permitting. Subject to alteration without notice)

EVERY DAY (SUNDAYS INCLUDED)
UNTIL SUNDAY, 19th SEPTEMBER, 1961
All Fares include Pier Tolls paid by the Company

		FARES Single	Day Excursion
1-15 p.m. *ST. TUDNO* or *ST. SEIRIOL*	MENAI BRIDGE (1 hour ashore) Through picturesque Menai Strait. Due, 2-40 p.m. Return, 3-45 p.m. Due Llandudno, 5-0 p.m.	6/-	8/6
	CIRCULAR TOUR Out by boat, return by any Crosville bus.	—	10/- Children 5/-
	Out by boat, return by rail (any train).	—	10/2 Children 5/1
5-15 p.m. *ST. TUDNO* or *ST. SEIRIOL*	LIVERPOOL Due 7-40 p.m.	13/-	Period 20/-

SUNDAYS

		Single	Day Excursions
10-45 a.m. *ST. TRILLO*	MORNING CRUISE Viewing the Great Orme and Puffin Island. Due back, 12-15 p.m.	—	4/6
2-30 p.m. *ST. TRILLO*	MENAI BRIDGE A delightful cruise through Menai Strait. Due, 4-00 p.m. Return, 4-30 p.m. Due Llandudno, 6-00 p.m.	6/-	8/6
6-00 p.m. *ST. TRILLO* 18th June to 3rd September	EVENING CIRCULAR TOUR Through Menai Strait to Menai Bridge. Due, 8-0 p.m. Return by Crosville bus. Post Office Square 8-30, 8-48 p.m. Due Llandudno 10-25, 10-25 p.m.	6/-	8/- Children 4/6
7-30 p.m. *ST. SEIRIOL* or *ST. TRILLO*	GRAND EVENING CRUISE Towards Puffin Island. Due back 9-0 p.m.	—	5/-

MONDAYS

9-30 a.m. *ST. SEIRIOL* 19th June to 4th September	LIVERPOOL (Two hours ashore) Due, 12-00 noon. Return from Liverpool, 2-00 p.m. Due Llandudno, 4-30 p.m.	—	10/-
10-45 a.m. *ST. TRILLO*	MENAI BRIDGE (Isle of Anglesey) 3½ hours ashore to visit beauty spots. Return: St. Trillo 12-45 p.m., St. Tudno 3-45 p.m. Due Llandudno: St. Trillo 2-15 p.m., St. Tudno 5-00 p.m.	6/-	8/6
2-45 p.m. *ST. TRILLO*	AFTERNOON CRUISE To Puffin Island and towards Red Wharf Bay. Due back, 4-45 p.m.	—	6/6
6-00 p.m. *ST. TRILLO*	EVENING CIRCULAR TOUR Through Menai Strait to Menai Bridge. Due, 8-00 p.m. Return by Crosville bus. Post Office Square 8-30, 8-48 p.m. Due Llandudno 10-25, 10-23 p.m.	6/-	8/- Children 4/6

Children over three and under fourteen years, half fare.
Buffets and refreshment bars on all vessels.
Lunches and teas available on St. Tudno and St. Seiriol only.
Weekly Season Tickets (not transferable) 42/- (pier tolls excluded) issued from any date and available all advertised sailings of the Company's vessels from Llandudno. Not available on circular tours.
FOR FURTHER INFORMATION APPLY TO:
Llandudno: Company's Representative, Pier Gates. (Tel. Llandudno 76837).
Colwyn Bay: Crosville Motor Services (Tel. 2230). Pickford's Ltd., 26 Abergele Road (Tel. 2852).
Abergele: R. A. Roberts, Amity House. Rhyl: Crosville Motor Services (Tel. 437).
Beaumaris: G. M. Evans, Medical Hall, Church Street (Tel. 39).
Bangor: Crosville Motor Services (Tel. 2448).
Menai Bridge: Pier Gates Office (Tel. 12).
Caernarvon: Pritchard Bros., Porth-yr-Aur (Tel. 219).
Conway: G. N. Cooper, Ye Corner Cafe, Lancaster Square.
Railway Stations, or the Liverpool and North Wales Steamship Co. Ltd., 40 Chapel Street, Liverpool, 3 (Tel. CENtral 1653/4).
TICKETS AT COMPANY'S OFFICE, PIER GATES, LLANDUDNO, AND ... BRIDGE, FROM AGENCIES OR ON BOARD ...

TUESDAYS
All Fares include Pier Tolls paid by the Company

10-15 a.m. *ST. SEIRIOL* 20th June to 5th Sept.	DOUGLAS (Isle of Man) Due, 1-40 p.m. Return, 4-30 p.m. About 2¾ hours ashore—due back, 8-0 p.m. Bus tour from Peveril Square. Tickets from the Purser, 2/3.		
10-45 a.m. *ST. TRILLO*	MENAI BRIDGE (Isle of Anglesey) 3½ hours ashore to visit beauty spots. Return: St. Trillo 12-45 p.m., St. Tudno 3-45 p.m. Due Llandudno: St. Trillo 2-15 p.m., St. Tudno 5-00 p.m.		
2-45 p.m. *ST. TRILLO*	AFTERNOON CRUISE To Puffin Island and towards Red Wharf Bay. Due back, 4-45 p.m.		
6-00 p.m. *ST. TRILLO*	EVENING CIRCULAR TOUR Through Menai Strait to Menai Bridge. Due, 8-00 p.m. Return by Crosville bus. Post Office Square 8-30, 8-48 p.m. Due Llandudno 10-25, 10-23 p.m.	6/	

WEDNESDAYS

10-15 a.m. *ST. SEIRIOL* 21st June to 6th Sept.	DOUGLAS (Isle of Man) Due, 1-40 p.m. Return, 4-30 p.m. About 2¾ hours ashore—due back, 8-00 p.m. Bus tour from Peveril Square. Tickets from the Purser, 2/3.	17/6	
10-45 a.m. *ST. TRILLO*	MORNING CRUISE Viewing the Great Orme and Puffin Island. Due back, 12-15 p.m.	—	
2-30 p.m. *ST. TRILLO*	MENAI BRIDGE A delightful cruise through Menai Strait. Due, 4-00 p.m. Return, 4-30 p.m. Due Llandudno, 6-00 p.m.	6/-	
7-30 p.m. *ST. TRILLO*	GRAND EVENING CRUISE Towards Puffin Island. Due back, 9-00 p.m.	—	5

THURSDAYS

9-30 a.m. *ST. SEIRIOL* 22nd June to 31st August	LIVERPOOL (Two hours ashore) Due, 12-00 noon. Return from Liverpool, 2-00 p.m. Due Llandudno, 4-30 p.m.	—	10/
10-45 a.m. *ST. TRILLO*	MENAI BRIDGE (Isle of Anglesey) 3½ hours ashore to visit beauty spots. Return: St. Trillo 12-45 p.m., St. Tudno 3-45 p.m. Due Llandudno: St. Trillo 2-15 p.m., St. Tudno 5-0 p.m.	6/-	8/6
2-45 p.m. *ST. TRILLO*	AFTERNOON CRUISE To Puffin Island and towards Red Wharf Bay. Due back, 4-45 p.m.	—	6/6
6-00 p.m. *ST. TRILLO*	EVENING CIRCULAR TOUR Through Menai Strait to Menai Bridge. Due, 8-0 p.m. Return by Crosville bus. Post Office Square 8-30, 8-48 p.m. Due Llandudno 10-25, 10-23 p.m.	6/-	8/- Children 4/6

FRIDAYS

10-45 a.m. *ST. TRILLO*	MORNING CRUISE Viewing the Great Orme and Puffin Island. Due back, 12-15 p.m.	—	4/6
2-30 p.m. *ST. TRILLO*	MENAI BRIDGE A delightful cruise through Menai Strait. Due, 4-00 p.m. Return, 4-30 p.m. Due Llandudno, 6-00 p.m.	6/-	8/6
6-00 p.m. *ST. TRILLO*	EVENING CIRCULAR TOUR Through ...		

This wonderfully nostalgic photograph taken by the author's father George Danielson, is dated July 1972. Seven out of eight passenger ships (the entire fleet except for the **Manx Maid***) is assembled in Douglas Harbour. The line up from left to right is the* **Manxman, Mona's Isle, King Orry, Snaefell, Mona's Queen** *and* **Tynwald. The Ben-my-Chree** *is arriving in harbour and is seen in the centre foreground. (photo: George Danielson)*

On 11th and 12th January 1974 the **Ben-my-Chree** *encountered dreadful conditions off the coast of the Island. Captain J.R. Kinley was master and on the night of 11th January 1974 he had spent the whole night trying to find some shelter from the S.E. severe gale force 11 winds. The following week Captain Jack Ronan took over the "Ben" and found that conditions were still appalling.*

(photos: Noel Howarth)

The car ferry service to Dublin was inaugurated by the ***Mona's Queen*** on 3rd July 1974 but "duty free" was not permitted until 1st March 1978. The previous month she had also sailed to Dublin when a reception was held aboard to herald the new service. Initially duty free sales were achieved by having a mobile duty free caravan that was driven onto the car ferry taking the Dublin sailing. Later, the Customs and Excise let it be known that they required something more permanent to be built into two of the ships but thereafter, the use of the caravan was noted from time to time when necessary, depending on the ship in use.

The 1974 summer season ended with appalling September weather and the threat of a seamens' strike necessitating an all out effort to return passengers to the mainland in weather described in official channels as the worst ever on record for the time of year.
It would not be difficult to imagine how everyone aboard the **Mona's Queen** *felt at the moments that these dramatic shots were taken by Noel Howarth, a professional local photographer of considerable skill. The* **Mona's Queen** *is seen going astern out of Douglas, rolling uncontrollably.*
(photos: Noel Howarth)

This photograph by Ray Pugh shows what can happen when a ship is hit by a freak wave. Twenty miles out of Liverpool at about 18.30 on 7th September 1974 in conditions that Captain C.H. (Harvey) Collister later described to the author as being "very poor" the **Ben-my-Chree** *was struck by a very large wave which broke over the port bow of the ship shattering the teak doors of the wheelhouse and damaging the forward end of the promenade deck where its bulkhead formed a walkway forward of the main superstructure. He ordered the ship to heave-to whilst the vessel was made secure and then proceeded on to Douglas. (photo: Ray Pugh)*

Captain Collister was a first class ship master (later marine superintendent) and helped the author greatly on occasions with his marine journalistic and photographic endeavours. Describing the 7th September incident some time later, whilst in between round trip sailings, Captain Collister hand-rolled a thin cigarette and drawing heavily on it, remarked calmly that "it's all in a days work, the ship is very strong and she was fine". Were it not for his own modesty, he might have mentioned that in fact, the wind was near hurricane force 11 and that sea conditions were positively dreadful!

Another Ailsa Shipbuilding Co. Limited brochure entitled "Craftsmen of the Clyde" and featuring the **Mona's Queen** *on its cover was used at the time of the* **Lady of Mann** *order being carried out. (archive material: Author's collection)*

Despite the earlier problems encountered with the new ***Mona's Queen***, the Steam Packet Company decided that a similar ship would be ordered as the Company's fourth car ferry. The decision was made in August 1973 with a view to delivery in the Spring of 1976. Whilst it had been intended to maintain the fleet of passenger ships in 1975 pending the arrival of the new car ferry, in fact the ***Tynwald*** was found to have serious turbine defects and she was offered for sale for scrap in October 1974. At the end of 1974, quickly after the news that the ***Tynwald*** was to be withdrawn and with the expected arrival of the new car ferry in 1976, the decision was taken to dispose of another passenger ship at the end of the 1975 season. The ***King Orry*** was in generally worse condition than her peers, no doubt on account of the long years of winter work she undertook and as a result, she too was earmarked for disposal.

Ailsa Shipbuilding were, once again successful with their tender for the new car ferry and as construction proceeded it became known that on 4th December 1975, the new ship would be named ***Lady of Mann*** by Mrs. Keith Rae, wife of one of the directors.

The Lady of Mann

In this 1975 aerial view of Ailsa Shipbuilding's yard at Troon, we see the **Lady of Mann** *on the stocks under construction and in the foreground, the Steam Packet Company's freighter* **Conister,** *undergoing overhaul.*
(photo: Author's collection)

Inset: The **Lady of Mann** *on the slipway under construction at Troon. Note the main engines are installed at an early stage of the ship's building and that windows are cut out after the main superstructure has been fabricated and welded together.* *(photos: Author's collection)*

Right: This classic 1970s photograph shows the **Ben-my-Chree** *at Liverpool on a wet and blustery day. Alongside the old floating landing stage, with its rotting wooden planking much in evidence, are the Rea tugs* **Cedargarth** *and* **Maplegarth** *and ahead of them is the Alexander Towing tug* **Canada** *and one of her sisters* **Formby** *or* **Gladstone.** *(photo: Ray Pugh)*

For her 1976 overhaul the **Mona's Queen** *went to Manchester. This necessitated the tops of her masts being cut away to enable her to pass under the bridges of the Manchester Ship Canal.*
(photo: V. Gillibrand)

At the invitation of Captain P.C. (Peter) Corrin (now the marine superintendent) and Mr. M.R. (Mike) Casey (fleet engineer), the author made the trip up the ship canal aboard the ***Peveril*** for her 1983 overhaul. The voyage ranks as one of the most interesting in his 40 years of making such trips which have included the whole range from luxury cruises in the ***Canberra*** to lazy trips in cargo boats around the Western Isles of Scotland and everything in between. The very first such trip was in 1954 aboard the Southampton paddle steamer ***Princess Elizabeth***, a trip so rough that it made the front pages of the national newspapers. That voyage, undertaken at the ripe age of just eight years, resulted in the author immediately writing his first piece about sea travel and clearly marks the beginning of what has become a lifetime interest.

The ***Mona's Queen*** inaugurated car ferry sailings to Fleetwood with the first sailing on 15th June 1976 but whilst dredging operations remained necessary, the tides caused some interference with schedules. She had visited Fleetwood a year earlier on a routine sailing and thus became the company's first car ferry to do so. At the time she had carried out ramp tests in readiness for the new service proposed for and duly commenced in 1976.

The launch of any ship is a major event and living on an island renders the arrangements all the harder to organise. Here we see the programme of events, itinerary and invitations to the launch of **Lady of Mann** *and the celebration dinner that followed. These are in the name of Captain and Mrs. A.W.G. Kissack, Capt. Kissack was by then marine superintendent. Shortly after his retirement, he was ordained as a priest thus exchanging his marine pilot's licence to become the proverbial sky pilot.*
(archive material: Capt. Westby Kissack)

The Chairman and Directors of
The Isle of Man Steam Packet Company Limited
request the pleasure of the company of
Captain & Mrs. A. W. G. Kissack
at the Marine Hotel, Troon, Ayrshire
on Wednesday, 3rd December, 1975

R.S.V.P. Secretary,
Imperial Buildings,
Douglas, Isle of Man.

Dinner 7 for 7-30 p.m.
Lounge Suits

The Chairman and Directors of
Ailsa Shipbuilding Company Limited
request the pleasure of the company of
Captain & Mrs. A.W.G. Kissack
on Thursday, 4th December, 1975, at noon.
to witness the Launch of
M.V. "LADY OF MANN"
for the Isle of Man Steam Packet Company Limited
and thereafter to Luncheon
in the Marine Hotel, Troon
The Naming Ceremony will be performed by
Mrs. J. E. K. Rae

R.S.V.P. to the Secretary

Shipyard,
Troon, Ayrshire
November, 1975

LAUNCH — M.V. "LADY OF MANN"
4th DECEMBER, 1975

PROGRAMME

11.15	Cocktails in the Board Room of Ailsa Shipbuilding Co. Limited, Troon.
Noon	Naming Ceremony of "Lady of Mann" by Mrs. J. E. K. Rae.
12.30 for 13.00	Luncheon at Marine Hotel, Troon, as guests of the Company.

ALL TRAFFIC CARRIED SUBJECT TO THE STANDARD CONDITIONS OF CARRIAGE OF THE COMPANY AS EXHIBITED IN ITS OFFICES AND ON BOARD ITS VESSELS

The Isle of Man Steam Packet Co. Limited
(INCORPORATED IN THE ISLE OF MAN.)

TELEGRAMS "STEAMERS, DOUGLAS."
TELEPHONE No. DOUGLAS 3824
TELEX 62414 STEAMERS, DOUGLAS

P.O. BOX No. 5
Imperial Buildings,
Douglas, Isle of Man.

OUR REFERENCE
YOUR REFERENCE

November, 1975.

TRAVEL ARRANGEMENTS, ETC., FOR GUESTS TRAVELLING FROM ISLE OF MAN TO TROON FOR LAUNCH OF LADY OF MANN

Wednesday, 3rd December

2.00 p.m.	Depart Ronaldsway in chartered Dart Herald of B.I.A. Passengers are requested to arrive Airport by 1.30 p.m.
2.45 p.m.	Arrive Prestwick and transfer to Marine Hotel, Troon. (Accommodation reserved).
4.00 to 4.30 p.m.	Afternoon Tea.
7.00 p.m.	I.O.M.S.P.Co.Ltd. Cocktail Party.
7.30 p.m.	I.O.M.S.P.Co.Ltd. informal dinner (no speeches).

Thursday, 4th December

11.00 a.m.	Leave Hotel for Yard of Ailsa Shipbuilding Co.
11.15 to 11.45 a.m.	Cocktails in Board Room.
12 noon	Name and launch vessel.
12.15 p.m.	Transfer to Marine Hotel for luncheon as guests of Builders of vessel.
5.15 p.m.	Leave Hotel for Prestwick.
6.00 p.m.	Leave Prestwick in chartered Dart Herald of B.I.A.
6.45 p.m.	Arrive Ronaldsway.

Even after her launching, fitting out of the ***Lady of Mann*** was delayed and she too missed the forthcoming T.T. traffic for which she had been expressly ordered. Once again, the remaining old passenger steamers were pressed into carrying more cars and this was particularly distressing on the Dublin route where the two year old car ferry service was very much the flagship service.

The **Lady of Mann** *was finally ready to run her sea trials on the Skelmorlie mile on 24th June 1976 and still some final adjustments were necessary before the formalities could be completed and certificates issued.* *(photo: Author's collection)*

The ship was handed over at Troon on 29th June 1976 and sailed for Douglas at 14.15 where she arrived that evening. She is seen here passing Maughold Head for the first time, en route from Troon.
(photo: George Danielson)

The brand new **Lady of Mann** *at Douglas waiting to take her maiden voyage from Douglas to Liverpool on 30th June 1976.* *(photo: Author)*

Following the arrival of the **Lady of Mann,** *on 30th June 1976 the four car ferries settled down into a regular sailing pattern for two years but only until the rival Manx Line set up in business using the ro-ro multipurpose ferry* **Manx Viking.** *Here we see the* **Mona's Queen** *departing from Douglas in a summer storm with arch rival* **Manx Viking** *still in her original Manx Line colours waiting to enter harbour. These photographs by the author appeared in his regular shipping series "Scene Afloat" in the Isle of Man Weekly Times and local papers circulating on the mainland fifteen years ago.*
(photos: Author)

On 26th August 1978, the rival Manx Line operated its first sailings between Heysham and Douglas where they had constructed the Island's first linkspan for their own exclusive use. Shortly thereafter, the new company was found to be in financial difficulties following which it was taken over by James Fisher & Son Ltd. of Barrow-in-Furness and later by the railway owned shipping subsidiary, Sealink. Hopefully, one day Capt. Andrew Douglas, who is now the editor of *Sea Breezes*, will write the Manx Line story for which, as its founding port manager and marine superintendent, he is uniquely qualified. The arrival of Manx Line on the scene had repercussions on the Steam Packet Company as the old Manx company would, in the end, prove to be unable to beat off the Sealink opposition which was backed by deeply lined British Government pockets.

The Steam Packet Company's coveted independent existence suddenly looked in danger but a formal merger of the two interests was still some years off and its final take-over was resisted until 29th March 1996.

Undoubtedly the Manx Line interlude brought about the early demise of several of the Steam Packet Company's ships including some of the main subjects of this book but like it or not, a lot of valuable lessons were learnt from this period. However reluctantly it may have appeared, the rival company quickly brought the Isle of Man Steam Packet Company into the 20th century.

The year 1980 started off very stormy and in this series of photographs taken on 21st January that year, the **Ben-my-Chree** *is seen departing from Douglas on the morning sailing. Even before the ship has cleared the harbour wall her stern has dropped into a deep trough and all but a few hardened sailors will already be hoping to survive the next four or five hours without succumbing to sea sickness. In those early days, the procedure was to leave Douglas Harbour going astern and then to heave-to in the Bay whilst the bow rudder was secured in the central position following which the vessel could get underway again and set course for Liverpool. In really bad weather, the resulting slow turn into the oncoming heavy seas frequently caused violent pitching, rolling and often a corkscrewing movement as the ship had no way on her and the stabilisers were therefore totally ineffective. There she would wallow at the mercy of the gale until the propellers began to bite and the ship started to make some headway, much to the relief of all aboard.*

(photos: Author)

Above: A lively photograph of the **Mona's Queen**, *scudding into Douglas from Liverpool on 14th October 1980. Standing on the end of the Battery Pier, well before any ship arrived, it was possible to see the wall of water being pushed along ahead of the arriving vessel.*
(photo: Author)

Right: During the busy summer season the ships still managed to get a day off from time to time for routine maintenance. Here we see the **Manx Maid** *having been hosed down from stem to stern with all her sliding doors open to assist drying her teak decks. The* **Manxman** *is on the north side of the Victoria Pier having just arrived from Liverpool.* *(photo: Author)*

The **Manx Maid** *sets off to Liverpool into the teeth of a full south easterly gale. Prior to the building of the Battery Pier extension in 1982, in conditions such as these, Douglas harbour sometimes had to be closed to shipping on account of the severe weather. When gale force winds were in the east the harbour at Douglas could be exceptionally rough making it virtually impossible to discharge with the ship heaving up and down violently.* *(photo: Author)*

In easterly gales when Douglas harbour was closed, the ships used to divert to Peel. If the diversion was known early enough, the journey was only a little longer than normal. However, quite often the ship would be either off Douglas or well on her way when the decision to close the harbour was taken necessitating a wearisome extension to the storm battered ship and her passengers. These three excellent photographs of the **Manx Maid** *at Peel in winter 1980/81 were taken by Eddie Fryer, a resident of the famous sunset city. In these photographs, the light was very low and ten years before it became the vogue, by having a long exposure, the photographer has managed to encapsulate some movement in the red ensign flying at the stern of the ship. Eddie is an excellent photographer of a wide range of subjects, including the famous snow capped mountains and hills of Nepal, the Far East and the arid desserts of North Africa where he walks extensively. He is a regular judge at island photographic competitions.*

(photos: E.A. Fryer)

MANX MAID
DOUGLAS

Some Memories and Personal Reflections

The following is a selection of pieces chosen to highlight some of the wide range of topical correspondence, interesting discussions and lighter moments enjoyed and shared by people who for one reason or another, professional or personal, have been close, not only to the Steam Packet Company but, also to the **Manx Maid**, *the* **Ben-my-Chree**, *the* **Mona's Queen** *and the* **Lady of Mann** *in particular.*

Lowey's Removals

The business of shipping loose goods to the Isle of Man (and elsewhere) on the decks of passenger steamers was economically viable on account of the fact that it obviated the need for empty return trips for lorries, wagons or lift vans, the forerunner of the modern day container.

Mr. and Mrs. Kefford's business, which started in Mrs. Kefford's side of the family in 1878 began as a removal firm and a little later, also a second hand shop selling furniture, china and other items they bought at auction. They operated from premises in the Toxteth, Dingle and Aigburth areas of Liverpool.

Although bombed during the war and all their windows were blown out, Lowey's premises fared better than many but after the war, compulsory purchase of the Toxteth property in 1956 caused the business to be moved wholly to Aigburth Vale.

Although they had been doing some house removals to and from the Island prior to this, Lowey's shipping of furniture to the Isle of Man commenced when European furniture manufacturer, Harris Lebus, expanded its markets beyond the major Liverpool department stores like Owen Owens, T.J. Hughes' and Lewis's to the more remote shopping areas, including those in the Island.

The arrangement was that when the Steam Packet boats were quiet, that is to say throughout the winter and on afternoon sailings in the season, Lowey's porters would load items of furniture and other loose goods, later complete kitchens and bathrooms, and stow them aboard the decks of the steamer for the crossing to Douglas. With the advent of the car ferries, more and more goods were carried this way and part of the car deck was reserved for "goods on deck". Suppliers from all over Europe were delivering goods for shipment to the Island, into Lowey's depot in Aigburth Vale, sufficient to warrant a delivery lorry attending the boat virtually every day. Latterly, regulations made it necessary for dock labour to physically carry the goods aboard but Lowey's continued to stack and secure it, to ensure arrival in good condition.

A major customer of this service was the famous bathroom and kitchen centre A. Skillicorn Ltd. of Laxey which in those days was also a busy plumbers merchants. The Principal of that business, Trevor Skillicorn has been a good friend of the author and his family for twenty-five years. As is so often the case, it was the author's chance comment to Trevor Skillicorn that elicited a fascinating discussion about Lowey's shipping and forwarding agency, production by the author of the relevant photographs from his collection, and this section of the memoirs was the result!

Others who shipped using Lowey's agency included T.H. Corkhill, Paradise and Gell, Taggarts, James Caine, J.T. Clucas, A.W. Black & Sons, The Home Improvement Centre and Tods Ltd.

Trevor Skillicorn's recollection of the service was that in the summer, it was often 8pm in the evening before they could make a start to unload their goods after the boat had arrived from Liverpool and discharged passengers and cars. If they were lucky and the tide was not too far out this could be accomplished relatively easily although a typical message from Lowey's would read "43 pieces of furniture", so a lot of hard manual work was still called for. Things were rather different at low spring tides when superhuman effort was demanded. When the tide dropped too low or when the car ramps had to be withdrawn for the night, the only way to complete the unloading was to manhandle the goods up the steep narrow gangplank. It was often 11pm at night before the job was done as it could require, in the case of Skillicorn's business, several trips to and from Laxey to store the goods and to re-load with more from the car deck of the ferry.

Following the Steam Packet Company's move to Heysham in 1985 and the advent of roll on – roll off, door to door carriers began to emerge in large numbers. This seriously eroded the business on offer to Lowey's but they carried on for another eight years using two articulated trailers which the Steam Packet Company purchased and regularly hauled into Lowey's depot for them to load. At Douglas, the trailers would arrive at the

Steam Packet warehouse where shops and traders would collect their own particular items. At about this time a local firm called Manx Move operated a link service between Lowey's depot, providing door to door van delivery in the Island, which service was much appreciated.

Mr. and Mrs. Kefford retired in 1993 and Lowey's business came to an end after 115 exemplary years of removal and shipping service. Without a doubt there was a synergy between their business, the Steam Packet Company's steamers and Island businesses all of which were able to benefit from the interaction of each upon the other.

Lowey's removal van attends the **Mona's Queen** *in Liverpool, one day in November 1984. Note the ship's lifeboats slung out in the davits.*
(photo: Author)

Captain W E (Ernie) McMeiken

"I think it was the month of July 1971 when, as master of the ***Ben-my-Chree*** and on passage from Liverpool to Douglas I received a radio message from Head Office, Imperial Buildings in Douglas informing me that after arrival in Douglas and with passengers landed, we would be departing light ship immediately for Ardrossan. Arriving at Victoria Pier, Douglas, passengers and cars were soon discharged and we sailed as planned for the Clyde port. It transpired that the ro-ro vessel ***Lion*** owned by Burns & Laird Line (part of the Coast Lines group) on its daily sailing from Ardrossan to Belfast had sustained a serious mechanical breakdown and was taken off service.

As the "Ben" was now chartered by Burns & Laird Line to operate this service, it gave us a wonderful opportunity to show our new boat off and her capacity for carrying vehicles.

It was a quiet trip from Douglas to Ardrossan and with no passengers on board it gave us a chance of making up for lost time, to wash down and spruce ourselves up. We arrived at the berth at Winton Pier at about 20.00 where we were met by the Agent of the Steam Packet Company and the local Agent from Burns & Laird Line. Sunday was a beautiful day and the crew of the "Ben" were all on top line. We began loading at 08.30, accepting any and all traffic for shipment and the passengers made themselves comfortable and we sailed at 10.00. As mentioned before, it was such a nice day, calm and warm, our course took us clear of Ailsa Craig from where we were seeing the Irish coast, twenty miles away.

Approaching Black Head, which is at the northern entrance to Belfast Lough, we endeavoured to contact Belfast Port control.

This we eventually did after we opened the Lough and cleared Black Head and

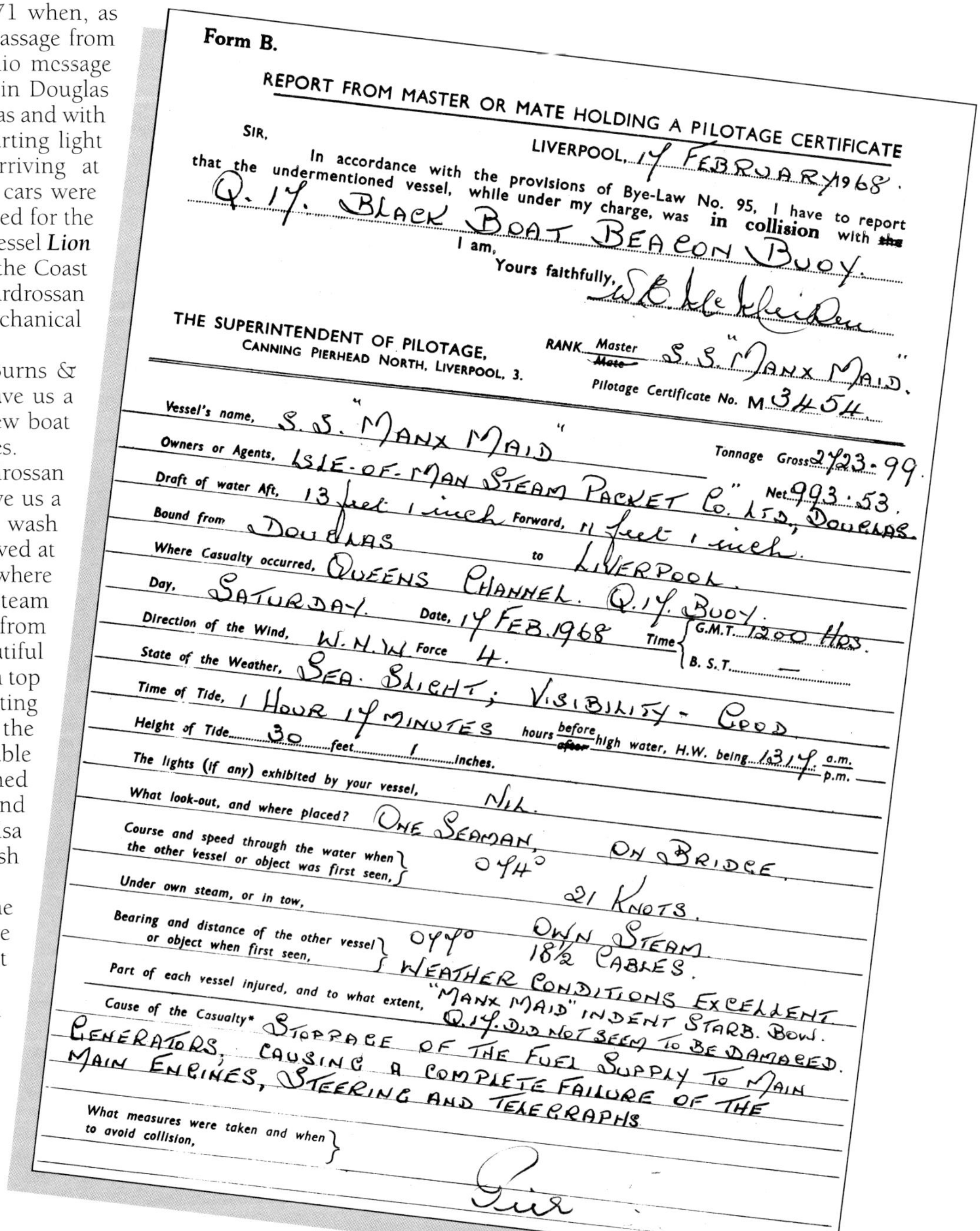

Form B.

REPORT FROM MASTER OR MATE HOLDING A PILOTAGE CERTIFICATE

SIR,

LIVERPOOL, 17 FEBRUARY 1968.

In accordance with the provisions of Bye-Law No. 95, I have to report that the undermentioned vessel, while under my charge, was **in collision** with ~~the~~ Q. 17. BLACK BOAT BEACON BUOY.

I am,

Yours faithfully,

W.E. McMeiken

THE SUPERINTENDENT OF PILOTAGE,
CANNING PIERHEAD NORTH, LIVERPOOL, 3.

RANK Master ~~Mate~~ S.S. "MANX MAID."

Pilotage Certificate No. M 3454.

Vessel's name, S.S. "MANX MAID"

Owners or Agents, ISLE-OF-MAN STEAM PACKET Co. LTD, DOUGLAS.

Tonnage Gross 2723·99. Net 993·53.

Draft of water Aft, 13 feet 1 inch Forward, 11 feet 1 inch.

Bound from DOUGLAS to LIVERPOOL.

Where Casualty occurred, QUEENS CHANNEL. Q.17. BUOY.

Day, SATURDAY. Date, 17 FEB. 1968 Time G.M.T. 1200 HRS. B.S.T. —

Direction of the Wind, W.N.W. Force 4.

State of the Weather, SEA. SLIGHT; VISIBILITY - GOOD.

Time of Tide, 1 HOUR 17 MINUTES hours before ~~after~~ high water, H.W. being 1317 a.m. p.m.

Height of Tide 30 feet 1 inches.

The lights (if any) exhibited by your vessel, NIL.

What look-out, and where placed? ONE SEAMAN, ON BRIDGE.

Course and speed through the water when the other vessel or object was first seen, 074° 21 KNOTS.

Under own steam, or in tow, OWN STEAM.

Bearing and distance of the other vessel or object when first seen, 074° 18½ CABLES.

WEATHER CONDITIONS EXCELLENT.

Part of each vessel injured, and to what extent, "MANX MAID" INDENT STARB. BOW. Q.17. DID NOT SEEM TO BE DAMAGED.

Cause of the Casualty* STOPPAGE OF THE FUEL SUPPLY TO MAIN GENERATORS, CAUSING A COMPLETE FAILURE OF THE MAIN ENGINES, STEERING AND TELEGRAPHS

What measures were taken and when to avoid collision,

Right: Report from Capt. W. E. McMeiken concerning an incident involving the **Manx Maid** *and Q 17 Buoy on 17th February 1968.*

Burns & Laird Line's ferry the **Lion**.
(photo: Cammell Laird)

White Head, Port Control informed us of our discharging berth but they were surprised at our expected time of arrival which proved to be one hour ahead of the ***Lion's*** regular service time. After mooring at Albert Quay, our passengers had to wait patiently for transport as the local taxis and buses had not been notified of our early arrival.
This then was the pattern as we arrived an hour earlier in each port and continued on this footing for the remainder of our time on charter. In the ***Ben-my-Chree*** we made twelve trips, the ***Snaefell*** and the ***King Orry*** did six each whilst the ***Manxman*** did one.
There is a lot to be said for the consistency and reliability of this type of vessel and for the three years I was master of the ***Ben-my-Chree***, we never had any trouble whatever from the engines, or should I say turbines."
The above is taken from the written memoirs of former Steam Packet Commodore, Captain W E (Ernie) McMeiken, which he handed to the author during various evenings spent together discussing his interesting life at sea.

Captain T H (Tom) Corteen

During summer seasons, until shortly before his retirement in 1972, Captain Tom Corteen had been the last master of the famous old ***Lady of Mann*** (1930).
It is interesting to note that, when her previous master, Captain Lyndhurst (Lyndy) Callow retired two years previously, the future command of the ship was mentioned only in faint whispers as it was thought that no man could handle the difficult "Lady" properly ever again. Captain Tom Corteen proved them all wrong and like his predecessor, was able to handle the ship brilliantly. He was not a tall man and to see properly over her canvas dodgers and from her massive bridge cabs overhanging either side of the ship, he had a wooden step made to give some vital extra height. With such an improved view of his Lady's fine lines and extremities, no wonder she was ultimately referred to as "Toms Lady".
On one of many trips upon which the author took retired Captain Corteen to view the ships in the harbour, a voice was heard calling "Hello captain, remember me? I was your tiger on the Lady". A captain's *tiger* was his personal steward and it was really nice that after all those years, his tiger was still quick to recognise his old ship's master.
During fireside chats with the author, Captain Corteen told of hundreds of crossings he had made including very difficult ones to Barrow-in-Furness when wind and tide were against him. Some stories are on tape, preserved for all time. He likened the handling of all the ferries unto a flag flying at the mast-head in a strong wind. In the analogy, not unlike the flag, only one end of his ship was controlled by the ship's propellers and rudder whilst the other end had to be encouraged to maintain course especially at slow speed or when proceeding astern, despite wind and tide opposing him. "Tom's Lady", the old ***Lady of Mann***, was so powerful, he said, that he could drive her out of trouble using one engine ahead and screwing the ship round using the other full astern.
Approaching piers and harbours in anything like a gale often called for a very quick approach in order to keep the ship's head up. If the approach was too slow or wind and tide too great she would quickly pay off and end up so far from the pier that it was impossible to throw ropes. Too fast an approach was just as serious and in the steam powered ships the manoeuvre often called for a "double rap" on the engine room telegraph. This was a well used signal to the Chief Engineer to give full astern power with all possible haste. He and the master would both know that at that moment, ship and pier would be closing fast and that the engines would have to stop the ship in time to prevent a collision. In practice the procedure was as well tried and tested as it was exciting, and was often preceded with a cautionary 'phone call from the bridge to the engine room saying "I may have to give you a double rap".
In the ***Mona's Queen*** and the ***Lady of Mann*** with the inception of bridge control of the engines when manoeuvring, the " double rap" became a thing of the past.

Captain J E (Jack) Ronan – Standing-by

Captain J.E. (Jack) Ronan
(photo: Island Photographics)

"When the summer season finished it was only necessary to have two ships out for the winter service which meant the other vessels of the fleet had to lay-up in sheltered berths in certain ports and harbours. Of recent times that included Birkenhead and Barrow-in-Furness but previously a ship or sometimes two was laid up at the Tongue in Douglas but this practise stopped when the two funnelled ***Victoria*** was scrapped after the 1956 season.

While ships were in the principal places of laying-up, the Port Authority rules and bye-laws, not to mention the ship insurance conditions, required that there must be a certificated officer aboard at all times in case of fire, weather or other emergencies.

This meant that a mate and an engineer would be standing-by each vessel but sometimes there were more and occasionally one of us managed two ships.

Officially this was called standing-by but it passed into our language as lay-up.

It was not a popular duty as you were away from home for weeks on end, for example I have done eight weeks at a time at Barrow-in-Furness. There was a marked drop in pay and conditions, that is to say that in the depths of winter poor lighting and no cook, you really had to fend for yourself. It was a rather squalid existence but in fairness to the Steam Packet Company, it was no worse than any other company and it did at least provide some employment.

Throughout the worst of the winter, the lay-up officer was in reality lone ship keeper and fire watcher and not much else went on. In the spring, fitting out work would start again in readiness for the next season and the crews would begin working on the ships, making for a bit more life around.

My first experience of lay-up duty was in 1960, just before the arrival of the first car ferry, ***Manx Maid***. I was posted to Birkenhead to stand by the old ***Tynwald*** and on this occasion brought the family with me as our stay was expected to be a long one. The two older children started at Cathgart Street School but understandably, they did not like the upheaval and it must have been quite a shock for them coming from the relatively "well insulated" Isle of Man.

In winter, being nearest to the gangway, the mate generally had the third class or lower bar which was divided up into three sections with timber bulkheads creating a living area, bedroom and the scullery which was the actual bar itself. If the chief engineer was aboard he had the top, first class bar.

In the "living area", a stove was provided. It was coal fired bogie type known as a *Beetonette* or *Modern Mistress* and had Queen Anne type legs and its own funnel which went up through the deck. Every Saturday the stove had to be taken apart and thoroughly cleaned, polished and reassembled. Our hot water supply was limited to what we could heat up in buckets and pans. In this way we could have a bath by pouring the hot water into our tin bath which we would place in front of the stove and after a days work getting filthy, this was indeed a luxury.

On a Saturday we would then go off to market to buy the weeks supplies, and we might get to see a football match too.

In Barrow-in-Furness provided there was someone else aboard to cover the watch, there were some good walks to be had when the weather was fine. We often walked to Walney Island, Furness Abbey and sometimes got as far as Ulverston.

If there was any cash left over after buying the weeks food, we might go to the pictures and perhaps call in for a pint of beer after the show. I think we frequented the *Burlington* and the *Steamer,* whilst the engineers favoured the *Albion*.

We sometimes had a wireless set aboard but, being long before the days of transistor radios being popular and cheap, when the ships generators were shut down in the evening we had no power.

The only light we had was a very feeble 10 volt supply "borrowed" from the local railway yard adjacent and we regularly had to supplement this with oil lamps.

Birkenhead was a much more convenient place to lay up as you were only just across the river from the daily boat service to the Island and the great city of Liverpool.

In the late 1960s, I think all the ships laid up at Birkenhead except for the old ***Lady***

of Mann which often went to Barrow-in-Furness.
At Birkenhead, we would have four ships in the Morpeth Dock and one at Vittoria Wharf which would be the standby boat in case of emergencies.
I was chief officer of the ***Manx Maid*** in 1967 and she was laid up for the winter whilst the ***Manxman*** and the ***Ben my Chree*** provided the winter service. We were in the north east corner of the Morpeth Dock and as this was her first winter lay-up, accommodation had to be built for the mate in which he could live whilst aboard. The tradition of the chief officer staying aboard goes back years and whilst during the day there might be some engineers aboard, during the months of long dark winter evenings, he had to be self sufficient for light, heat and water.
By that time, I was something of an expert at the lay-up scene and designed an apartment or flat to my own specifications and, quite fastidiously, I supervised its construction knowing that I was the one who would have to live in it! The top bar was chosen being the only space of the required size and the Mate's apartment was duly constructed by carpenters sent out from Douglas for the purpose. By now the company did recognise that with a senior mate aboard, they were in effect "killing several birds with one stone". That is to say, in just one person they got their certificated officer to comply with port bye-laws, ship keeper, fire watcher and someone sufficiently self-contained not to have to have engineers and others aboard just to maintain his presence. It had all become really very efficient.
The crew of the ***Manx Maid*** not having been involved in laying-up procedures for some years, many may never have come across it before, were quite fascinated by my knowledge of the necessary preparations and they were quite amused as well. When the job was nearing completion, I happened to take some time off to present a box of kippers to the Blue Funnel Line foreman painter off whom we used to borrow painting scows which were worth their weight in gold when fitting out boats in the spring.
On my return to the ship an hour or two later I was asked by my second officer, Andrew Douglas (now editor of *Sea Breezes* magazine) to see something urgently in the newly built apartment. I flew up wondering what on earth could have gone wrong in such a short time of my being off the ship.
On entering the apartment, as by then the bar had been completely transformed into a "home from home", it was in complete darkness and I really feared the worst. Then, someone turned on the lights and all the crew were there clapping. It had been decked out with garlands and decorations and they had laid on a lovely buffet and party for me. Best of all, hanging from the deck head was a board on which were painted the words *Cronk Ronan*. This had been painted by Dennis Clague a seaman from Ramsey. I was completely overwhelmed by this show of affection and had been wondering for days previously whether I had upset the men as the seemed to be keeping to themselves rather more than usual.
I stood by the ***Manx Maid*** for most of that winter which turned out to be a bitterly cold one and so it was back to having two of the old bogie coal fires once again with the attendant mess of coal dust, ashes and grates to clean and polish.
That winter, my family joined me and six of us lived in that wooden apartment, named *Cronk Ronan*, built into the top bar of the car ferry, ***Manx Maid***. On Christmas Day we cooked Christmas dinner on the old coal fire and it tasted as good as any from a five star hotel. There were four other families in Birkenhead that Christmas, all of us looking after ourselves as best we could, so far from our beloved island and its home comforts."

Family entertainment! - Captain Jack Ronan's wife Betty oversees children Richard, Catherine, Billy and John painting the hawse pipes and anchor chains on the **Mona's Isle** *in Birkenhead, October 1966.*

Captain Jack Ronan – The worst ever voyage

The author also asked me to recount my worst ever trip in command of a Steam Packet ship. There have been many that could be described as very rough and a particularly bad one I had in the diminutive cargo boat ***Ramsey*** when we were caught out in a near hurricane that had not been properly forecast by the meteorological office. However, I think the following voyage is probably the worst of all.

"Between 8th and 13th January 1984 I was Pier Captain – a rather strange job involving being on the pier and seeing the ship in and out of harbour, advising the sailing master on weather conditions but generally, not doing a lot else. It was a job to do in winter when there were too many masters for the ships in service and leave and other jobs in the office had all been done.

On 14th January 1984, I joined the ***Lady of Mann*** at 01.30 as I considered it better to sleep on board the first night as the weather had been atrocious all week with further gales forecast. At 07.30 I started making calls as to the forecast. I was not too concerned about this end of the voyage but was anxious to get a local forecast from Mersey Radio for the period of our expected time of arrival. They were giving wind force 7, weather moderating before freshening again in the afternoon.

I had to make my decision as to whether to sail and at 07.40 with a heavy swell running outside the harbour after a week of gales, I decided to go, hoping the promised force 7 would hold out. We loaded with 150 passengers and 38 cars and at 08.42 departed from Douglas.

As soon as we cleared Douglas I could see the water was in turmoil from the storms of the past week so I decided to take her well down the Manx Coast. My idea being that from there I could make a run with the sea on my stern quarter making it a bit more comfortable for the ship and her passengers.

From Santon Head I set a course for Point Lynas on Anglesey hoping to pick up some calmer weather in the lee but by then, the wind had already risen to force 9. On that leg of the voyage, the "Lady" was running very well but with the ever rising storm, I could see the seas astern building up alarmingly. By the time we got off Anglesey I found there was to be no shelter at all and the storm had risen to force 10 later force 11, a near hurricane. The most frightening part was the run up the north Welsh coast from Point Lynas to the Bar light. My colleague Commodore Captain John Kennaugh had given me the tip that in really heavy following weather the ***Lady of Mann*** had to be kept going with full power and provided you did that, the "Lady" would manage to take care of herself and get us all safely to the other side.

I did just this and at full speed, we had the benefit of our stabilisers but on several occasions, my heart was in my mouth as she dug herself right under the huge seas. Here I have to give the "Lady" and her Ailsa shipbuilders full credit as, for every time she went right under, she rallied well and we made the Bar light, only 40 minutes late. I expected even worse conditions from the Bar to Formby, a notorious stretch of water at any time but with a near hurricane blowing full on the beam by rights it would be absolutely dreadful. In fact, the "Lady" steered and responded well despite the dreadful conditions. It was like a large weight being lifted from my shoulders but all the time it was in the forefront of my mind that I still had to tackle berthing at the landing stage.

At Liverpool I knew that the ***Mona's Queen*** had not ben able to sail and she was still moored in the south berth, her sailing cancelled through stress of weather. I was left with the task of trying to shoehorn the ***Lady of Mann*** into the north berth.

I realised that I would have a difficult job trying to swing round in the river and I could not even consider the question of tide as the normal swing to port was out of the question with all that weight of wind. First I tried to swing in the Alfred Dock entrance but "she would have none of it". I then proceeded off Cammell Lairds', south of Woodside as near in as I could get to try to find some lee. I managed to turn the ship there using full power and bow thrust. Then I headed toward the other side and the north berth of the landing stage. I decided I would tackle the approach as I would have in one of the old passenger steamers leaving plenty of distance between me and the landing stage to "see what she would do".

With a near hurricane on her exposed port side the "Lady" was coming in very quickly even with full power on the bow thruster and with main engines countering the wind. There was nothing else for it but to let go both anchors and hope that they would hold the ship as she came in. She took the stage quite heavily when we finally came alongside but no harm was done, at least not to the ship.

I was totally exhausted but perhaps this is hardly surprising as, after I had signed off with Mersey Radio, Liverpool Port Authority, they told me the wind speed was 60 knots. During the voyage, Mersey Radio had reported gusts of wind up to 100 knots. Whilst it was perfectly obvious what terrible conditions we were in with spume and spindrift as far as the eye could see, I broadcast this information to our passengers to keep them informed. Some of them kindly wrote to me and to the

Crew photograph taken aboard the **Mona's Queen** *In August 1988.*
Standing back row: Jim Fox 2nd Mate, Brian Goldsmith 2nd Eng., Don Nelson 3rd Eng., Kelly Greaser, Peter Gledhill Carpenter,
Middle rows: Ian Clarke Officers' Stwd, Tommy Harrison 1st Mate, Terry Clarke AB, Philip Kaye AB, Bridson Quartermaster, Willie Gelling 3rd Eng., Phil Davies Radio Officer,
Seated: Brian Johnson Chief Eng. Capt. J.E. Ronan, Brian Mallon Bosun, Bob Gerrard Purser.
(photo and detail : Capt Jack Ronan collection)

office after with plenty of kindly comments which helped to make it all the more worthwhile."

Readers might also like to know the sailors' colloquial description given when in heavy seas and the ship was hurrying along trying to keep to time, she was often said to be "Trampling the waves underfoot". This also described the need to keep going full ahead as much as possible as, at slower speeds, the stabilisers were not very effective."

RULES AND REGULATIONS FOR CAPTAINS, OFFICERS, ENGINEERS AND STEWARDS

RULE 78. The captain and the chief officer during their respective watches are to be careful to note that the side and masthead lights are constantly burning brightly at night.

The author's family experienced the corollary to this rule some years ago as guests of the commodore, Capt. John Kennaugh on the bridge of the* Tynwald*. The captain, who was renown for always being punctilious, had noted that the white light on the foremast had failed and before sailing, required the regulation emergency oil lamp to be taken from stores, filled, wick trimmed and lit prior to being hauled up the mast for the overnight voyage. It seems that it had been a very long time since anyone remembered having to do the exercise previously!

Capt T L Corkill

An interesting letter from Capt. T L Corkill (brother-in-law of Capt. Westby Kissack and Phyllis) marine superintendent in 1965 in response to an enquiry from a qualified master looking for work.

"Sir

I have received your letter of 16th inst. applying for a position as Deck Officer on one of this Company's vessels.

The passenger trade of this Company is concentrated mainly between June and September and for the remainder of the year, two passenger vessels maintain a daily service to and from Liverpool and six are laid up at Barrow-in-Furness and Birkenhead.

During busy periods it is common for the vessels to make two or more sailings in one day and extra remuneration is given when three or more trips are made on two consecutive days, National Maritime Board rate of pay applies at other times when on Articles.

When an Officer is standing by a vessel laid up and off Articles, approximately 80% of the pay on Articles is received plus 28/- (£1.40) subsistence.

Although many hundreds of thousands of passengers have disembarked and embarked at Douglas the harbour remains very open from N.N.E. through East to S.S.E. and often causes great anxiety, making it necessary for the ships to leave harbour until the weather improves.

Due to the peculiarities of our business all new entrants commence as Second Officers and for many years it has been the rule that the Second Officer steers the vessel into and out of all ports and estuaries.

If you are likely to visit the Island in the near future and wish to discuss the matter further, you could write and ask for an appointment."

Capt. T.L.Corkill

Lay-ups

Three views of the **Manx Maid** *and the* **Ben-my-Chree** *taken in November 1984, shortly after their withdrawal from service.*

(photos: Author)

Above: The **Mona's Queen**, *the troublesome* **Mona's Isle** *and the* **Lady of Mann** *laid up together in December 1985.*

(photo: Derek Medlock)

Left: The **Lady of Mann** *and the* **Mona's Queen** *on 3rd November 1991*
(photo: Gordon Ditchfield)

Above: The "Ben" in reflective mood on 9th March 1986.
(photo: Gordon Ditchfield)

Above: The **Mona's Queen** and the **Manx Maid** on 18th February 1984
(photo: John Collins)

Above: A beautiful sunset view of the **Manx Maid** and the **Manxman**. (photo: John Collins)

John Clarke

John and his wife Gladys have been known to the author for almost twenty-five years. John was a fireman on the ***Manx Maid*** and previously in the record breaking ***Viking*** (1905). In recent interesting and informative discussions, John described to the author, what life aboard was really like, particularly seen from the intimate perspective of one of the ship's firemen.

"We were always known as the "Down below crowd", there were seven or eight of us being four firemen, two greasers, one tunnel greaser/storeman and a spare man. The spare man relieved the others but his main duty was to look after the engineer officers' rooms as they has no stewards.

Our accommodation aboard the ***Manx Maid*** was right aft with its entrance seemingly amongst all the coils of mooring rope. The deck just there was a popular venue for the regular passengers, called the "contractors" who would gather there and talk amongst themselves and to us when we came up from below. Some of them liked to think of themselves almost as being part of the crew, they were really nice people and we got to know many of them very well.

Down below we had two small rooms in each of which, four of us slept. We had a toilet and shower and a galley in which our food was prepared and messrooms for ourselves and the seamen. One deck below us, there were three more rooms housing the twelve A.B.s carried in the ship and the donkeyman.

The donkeyman had an unusual existence because he was almost always working when every one else was off and vice versa. When the ship was alongside for the day he worked from 06.00 to 18.00 otherwise he came on duty before we sailed and when the boat docked. In days of old the donkeyman's job was to fire the donkey boiler which produced the steam for machinery aboard the ship when she was in harbour and running the main boilers would have been uneconomic. These days however his main tasks are centred around the night generator and the shore power line.

Until about the early 1970s the ships had no shore power when alongside so at night when the donkeyman stopped the generators, the ship was in total darkness. Things were much improved once we had shore power as then we had light all night. We would have a night watchman on deck. He was one of the twelve seamen we carried and every night a different one would stand the watch, generally ensuring that no one came aboard without permission, checking on mooring ropes and the like. If he was to be on watch at night, he got time off the previous and following day.

When we were overnight in Douglas most of the Manx officers and crews would go home soon after the ship arrived and the day's work was finished. After docking, the crew work involved carrying the mailbags ashore whilst the ropemen on the pier would come aboard to carry fresh produce, fruit and vegetables ashore which we carried on deck in large amounts. This was called "the grout".

We were expected back "all hands aboard by 07.00" for the next morning's sailing, in those days at 09.00. If South East wind was forecast, we would have to return to the ship and sleep aboard in case there was need to move the ship in the night if it became too rough in harbour.

Whilst on occasions we did have to leave harbour to seek shelter, often off Port Erin, Peel or Jurby, or anywhere we could find some lee, in fact this was a step taken only as a final resort by the master. This was because the risk of moving the ship out of harbour in gale force winds in the middle of the night was likely to be greater than the bumping that we might suffer staying in the harbour. On the other hand, the constant pounding the ship would suffer in very strong wind sending her crashing on and off the pier was very wearing and could cause structural damage if allowed to continue.

The seamen were divided into two watches. Half would attend to the bow ropes and half remained aft when leaving or arriving in port. As soon as we were clear of Douglas Head or the Bar light coming from Liverpool, we would set the ship's log over the stern and this provided a physical check on the distance travelled by the ship, a helpful aid to old fashioned but reliable "dead reckoning". These days much is done by satellite navigation systems but twenty or thirty years ago, speed, distance travelled and compass setting were all vital in ensuring the safe navigation of the ship.

Half of the seamen would stand down for the main part of the voyage and the others would each take turns at the helm, steering the ship and being look-out on the bridge. In fog we had extra look-outs and regulations required the bridge watch to sound the whistle at intervals of a minute. Down below, we kept all the watertight doors shut, so that in the unlikely event of collision damaging the ship, flooding would be controlled.

On the return trip, the other six seamen would swap over, each taking their turn at the wheel and look-out duty.

The use of the bow rudder, a helpful aid to navigation when running astern say backing out of Douglas, or going up to Belfast or Fleetwood was supervised by the ship's carpenter. He was not one of the "Down below crowd" nor an able seamen but had his cabin on deck along with the officers. The carpenter was also in charge of letting go the anchors.

There were three working firemen and one spare man (mentioned earlier). The firemen manned the port and starboard boilers which on the later ships were of the water tube variety. Supervising them was the leading hand, passing on the instructions regarding the amount of steam called for.

Abaft the boiler room were the engines where the two greasers worked with the engineers and further aft, the tunnel greaser's job was to ensure that the propeller shaft bearings ran cool, lubricating them as necessary.

As well as we firemen and greasers, there were engineer officers, in those days normally certificated for steam and often for motor too. The chief engineer was in charge but was in some ways a figure-head and dealt only with the most important matters, official paperwork, serious mechanical problems, ordering fuel etc., he usually was in the engine room when leaving and arriving in harbour. He left the daily running of the engines to his second in command, the second engineer. We also carried a third engineer and between the two of them and all of the "down below crowd", the engines were kept running as required.

Our fourth engineer came on duty at night and tended to overlap with the donkeyman to ensure continuity, but he rarely kept a watch at sea.

In summer we were often working several trips a day and in T.T. we worked round the clock. At other times when we were running a single trip to Liverpool, say, the famous 9 o'clock boat out of Douglas, we would arrive at around lunchtime and the rest of the time would be our own after the work for the day was done. The relevance of the saying "the 9 o'clock boat" derived from a local message for visitors who, if they complained about the island, were politely reminded that there was always the 9 o'clock boat the next morning.

Depending on which of the two boats that were in service you were on, you might have every weekend in Liverpool or in Douglas. At Christmas with the extra day off, the ship's rotas would swap round so that the other had the weekend in Liverpool which worked out fairly enough. That was aptly called "weekend away".

Some crew would stay aboard for the whole weekend as we had very little spare money and would read, play cards etc. We might go for a walk and a pint or two of beer at *John Halls* in the Dock Road, or *The Pig and Whistle* in town. A tremendous ability to sleep was developed by some who had seemingly nothing better to do. The "sleepers" could go to their bunk soon after docking on Saturday and not be seen again until sailing time on Monday! Others would go to see relatives, cross the river on the ferry to the Wirral but if a crew man was "going to see my auntie" it was not always quite what it seemed. For some it meant a visit to the secret girlfriend whilst for others, it was impossible for them to convince anyone that they really were going to visit their mother's or father's sister!

In our crew galley, which was coal fired, we would prepare our own food. We supplied it ourselves and then cooked and ate it. When we were in the busy season and not often or long in harbour, our wives and girlfriends would come down to meet the boat and give us baskets full of food they had bought or prepared for us. It was not until the late 1960s that what was referred to as "Company feeding" began. After that the company provided our victuals and a crew cook to prepare our meals for us.

The "kitty" was always a sore point. This was tips and money collected by the seamen for giving out the deckchairs and for handling passengers' suitcases into the baggage room. Those who can remember a chalk cross being marked on their case may not have realised that it meant the seamen had been tipped when the baggage was put in. Without a chalk cross, upon arrival at the destination port, the passenger was likely to be persuaded that a small donation would be in order! What made the kitty a sore point was that it was never shared with the firemen.

On day, so the story goes, one of the ships had touched bottom going up the Wyre to Fleetwood and gently resting on a sandbank waiting for the tide to rise, a fireman was heard to suggest in a deliberately loud whisper, that if the "kitty" was thrown overboard, just enough buoyancy might be obtained to get the ship back afloat! It is a good tale and certainly indicative of a certain amount of banter such practices can engender.

Voyages at night often used to be run very slowly and the engineers would take pride in calculating the engine revolutions precisely required to ensure that arrival at the destination next morning was on time with no necessity to hurry, or to slow down at the end of the trip. If six hours or more could be allowed for a given arrival time, the ship would be sailing so slowly it was called "Doodling Clink".

For much of the season when there was a midnight boat, not only did we carry mail but always the next days newspapers too. For years, a Mr.and Mrs. Chandler working for the newspaper wholesalers, used to go out from Douglas everyday on the 4 o'clock boat to Liverpool. At Liverpool the newspapers would come aboard and throughout the return journey, the couple would sort and stack the papers ready for delivery to the shops next morning. The system was very simple and worked extremely well".

Captain H N (Harry) Kinley

Capt. Harry Kinley and his family have long associations with the Isle of Man Steam Packet Company. His father was a sea captain and brother George, his elder by eight years, became Steam Packet commodore. One of his other brothers, William was father to both Vernon and Brian.

Vernon, Captain T.V. Kinley is mentioned throughout this book and is a present master of the **Lady of Mann** and assistant marine superintendent of the company. Captain W.B. (Brian) Kinley, Vernon's elder brother was a navigating officer with the Steam Packet Company but left them, becoming harbour master and finally the Isle of Man's chief harbour master before his recent retirement. The author greatly appreciates the efforts that these gentlemen have made on his behalf over the years. In harbour control at Douglas, high up above the sea terminal, Captain Brian Kinley was, as were the other harbour masters, always willing to be host to the author with the loan of a desk to work at and Lloyds Registers of Shipping to delve into.

Captain Harry Kinley was always known simply as "H.N.".

Prior to setting the scene for "H.N.'s" post war career, it is appropriate to recount briefly his wartime operations under naval orders.

When war was declared, Harry Kinley went with the old **Mona's Isle** (the former Southern Railway steamer **Onward** and a near sister of the Steam Packet Company's **Victoria**) to have guns mounted, prior to going south to join in the hostilities. The Manx ships being fast, were at that time running troops across the Channel sailing in convoy with destroyers.

As second officer under Capt. James Bridson he then joined the **Viking** which was very active in the evacuation of troops from Le Harve and later, Cherbourg. Aboard the **Viking**, Harry Kinley evacuated some of the civilians of Guernsey when France fell to the Germans and the Channel Islands were occupied. In one sailing, the **Viking** took almost the entire child population of Guernsey to Weymouth and the relative safety of the mainland.

In a recent long discussion the author enjoyed with Captain Kinley at his home in the south of the Island, he recounted that "our trip from St. Peter Port, Guernsey, was a very emotive departure with the parents of tearful children saying farewell to their offspring which were to be evacuated for the period of the war and no one knew how long that would be". Following that very important period, Harry Kinley was then recalled to Liverpool for the duration of the hostilities where his great experience as a Liverpool pilot was needed for the Atlantic convoys sailing in and out of the Mersey.

By 1962, Captain Harry Kinley was master of the coal-fired cargo vessel **Peveril.** He then worked his way on up through most of the old passenger ships before becoming master of the **Manx Maid** and finally the **Ben-my-Chree.**

"In those days", Captain Kinley recalled "when the ships were about to leave harbour, not only was the ship's whistle blown five minutes before departure but also the fo'c'sle bell was rung with increasing urgency as sailing time approached, as if to implore everyone who was intending to join the ship to hurry along".

On the subject of carrying cars and deck cargo, more about which appears in the opening chapter of the book, he said "Loading cars on the old passenger ships, had to be accomplished before any other passengers could board the ship. Even the vehicles had to be marshalled correctly, so that the Minis and other small cars went aboard first and were driven forward on the shelter deck where it narrowed immediately abaft the access door to the fo'c'sle.

Sometime this would annoy foot passengers quite a bit because they would be waiting to join the ship and could see all the activity with the cars being loaded and their occupants seemingly getting the best seats for the voyage. For many sailings drivers had to hold a first class ticket if they wished to bring their car".

At the gangway, until 1967 when the ships of the Steam Packet Company became single class, first and second class passengers would be separated with appropriate instructions as to the direction of their accommodation. At busy times when the crews were tired (and sometimes had been ashore for a quick drink or two) apparently this could be quite a procedure, as the directions were not always as polite as they might have been. Some men on gangway duty had their own choice of words for directing the passengers, not necessarily restricted to "first class to the right, steerage to the left".

The Judiciary of the Isle of Man had for many years, the power to order corporal punishment (birching) to violent young offenders and the worst cases were often deported immediately after.

In such instances, the Manx police would bring the culprits to the ship shortly before sailing time and hand them over into the custody of the master. Their treatment on the voyage varied between

After fifty years at sea, Captain Harry Kinley prepares for his last voyage in the **Ben-my-Chree**, *his favourite ship. He retired early in 1973.*

different ships and masters and also depending on their manner and behaviour when they were brought aboard.

If they were particularly contrite and sorry for their mis-behaviour they would be locked in a private cabin and generally looked after fairly well. Captain Harry Kinley had a way of dealing with those who were particularly recalcitrant as he would have the police escort lock them in the "birdcage" for safe keeping, well out of harms way.

"Down below we had what was called the "birdcage". A steel mesh pen in which we normally carried Royal Mail parcels and sometimes furniture and other items of value".

He always made a point of going to speak with his prisoners and to ensure that they had the basic essentials for the trip.

At the destination ports, they were often met by the police again who took the culprits off their hands, remarking that the Manx system of birching and instant deportation was a treatment they wished they had the power to administer.

Captain Kinley recalls another spectacle to be remembered as the ships were leaving harbour. "I would be on the bridge wing with both hands on the engine room telegraphs and giving orders to the man on the helm. My chief officer would be standing in the bows during the departure and by commands on his pocket whistle, all the ships flags, that is to say the stem jack, name flag, blue peter and any others we were flying, would all be ceremonially lowered in unison. Only the red ensign at the stern would remain flying for the crossing (and this could be dipped as a courtesy gesture to senior ships passing). It really was quite a sight".

In the author's discussions with captains Jack Ronan and Harry Kinley both recounted that "in the good old days" when the Steam Packet ships passed at sea, they would dip ensigns, particularly the senior ships. They rarely exchanged whistles, technically in case they were mistaken for advising changes of course although on occasions, often with a prior call on the V.H.F. radio, some loud salutes were enjoyed by all concerned. Sadly the traditional practise largely fell into disuse around late 1960s and early 1970s at which time crews and ships were no longer permanently attached.

"H.N." does not recall any child births aboard his commands although there were some obvious likely candidates that they watched rather anxiously throughout the voyage. He does remember a lady traveller to Fleetwood who had a troupe of performing dogs that had been to the Island to put on a show. Unfortunately, on the return trip one of the dogs was trodden on and retaliated as annoyed dogs sometimes do. The result was that the owner of the dog was badly bitten and Captain Kinley had to stitch up her foot as the ship had no medical personnel aboard. When they arrived alongside at Fleetwood, the casualty was taken for medical attention ashore. Apparently, the doctor said he could not improve on the first aid the Captain had administered and that she would now be quite alright until she arrived home and could see her own doctor.

Captain Kinley has much to say about all his years of service particularly sailings in and out of Fleetwood, a port he came to know very well. The older ships having no bow thrusters, normally used to turn round at the entrance to the River Wyre and sail astern up the Wyre Channel to Fleetwood. In bad weather this could be a horrible task with no shelter on the flying bridge (the monkey island) from where the master would navigate. Rain and gales were bad enough but with the wind against them too, oily black smoke, soot, hot ash and other emissions would often be blown from the funnel straight down onto the bridge making it impossible to breathe, let alone to see. The author recalls that on some trips, occasionally the old ship masters would proceed ahead all the way up to Fleetwood and would swing the ship by gently resting the bow on the sandy foreshore outside the North Euston Hotel and screwing the ship round on the engines. This was a useful manoeuvre but could only be done when the wind and state of the tide were right.

Fleetwood is a notoriously shallow twisting channel at low water. Harry Kinley remembers one inexperienced officer, who was making a Fleetwood trip for the first time, rushing into the wheelhouse to urgently inform him that there were sandbanks all along the port side of the ship. Captain Kinley calmly took him to the starboard side which was equally devoid of sea explaining that at low water, the muddy narrow channel ahead was supplying all the buoyancy the ship was going to get! "H.N." recounted to the author with obvious pleasure, his time with long serving bosuns George Davenport and Bruce Bridson (son of Captain P.J. (Ginger) Bridson).

Upon arrival at Fleetwood, just off Knott End jetty, there was a mussel bank which the ships had to skim over. As the depth of water dropped to virtually nothing, one could feel the ship loose her buoyancy before picking up again. Uncharitable commentators used to say that the port authority relied on the Steam Packet boats to help with the dredging of the channel as they swept by with their churning propellers scouring the mud from the bottom and it was then taken away with the tide!

Time off in Fleetwood for Harry Kinley was a happy event. "There my friend, the Fleetwood pilot, would lend me a bicycle and I would go for long rides. Over the Knott End ferry and north towards Glasson and all around the countryside there was very nice. At Knott End, if I was not sailing until next morning, I would probably go for a pint or two at a local public house there that I think was called the *Bowen Arms*. Staying on the Blackpool side there were plenty of sights to see and old haunts to revisit."

On 6th April 1972 (shortly before his retirement in 1973), Captain Kinley recalled that he had a sad drama aboard the ***Ben-my-Chree*** in which a seaman (not a crew member of the ship) went overboard. Captain Kinley was off the bridge at the moment the ship's general emergency signal was sounded by officer of the watch, Bob Adams. By interesting coincidence, Bob Adams had previously served his cadetship and time as a navigating officer with the author's brother Martin, who became a chief engineer with Clan Line before they both went their separate ways.

In the words of his own report (a copy of which Capt. Jack Ronan was able to supply, which exactly confirmed Harry Kinley's recollection of events), Captain Kinley was on the bridge within ten seconds. He then went through the whole text book procedure, by throwing a lifebuoy over the side to mark the location and he then turned the ship round and sailed the reciprocal course searching all the way. That day he had a number of the directors travelling aboard and the author's erstwhile good friend General Manager, Syd Shimmin too. Even though in the end, the lifeboat crew were not called upon to do so, they were in the boat and all ready to lower away in under four minutes following the emergency being sounded on the ship's whistle. "H.N." told the author that he always took great care to go through regular lifeboat drill and fire practise with all his crews so that when the need arose, they all knew exactly what was expected of them. He says they never let him down. On that particular day, after a lengthy search, it was agreed that there was no further chance of survival for the man overboard with the sea being so cold and rough and the ship returned to normal speed and course.

"H.N." is a fascinating man to talk to and with all his sea-going associations is a mine of information. His friends and family are very close and whilst sadly, his wife Eileen passed away five years ago he has daughter Elizabeth, son Peter and younger son Nelson (who is himself a deep sea marine radio operator) and the resulting six grandchildren and seven great-grandchildren all help to keep him very young at heart!

Bruce Purslow

Bruce Purslow, a former Marine Radio Officer with the Steam Packet Company was later employed as a Lecturer at Norwood Technical College, London where the author's father (to whom Bruce referred as "The Gov'nor") was Head of Radio and Telecommunications. He was a great friend of the author's family and of many Steam Packet men, particularly Capt. P J. (Ginger) Bridson.

At London, Bruce Purslow was able to renew his connection with the ***Glen Strathallan***, a trawler like private yacht, formerly owned by Douglas benefactor R.A. Colby Cubbon. He bequeathed the ship, and some money with which to operate her, through his mother who outlived him, to the Shaftsbury Homes for Youth Training. For many years Bruce Purslow had been a personal friend of the Cubbon family and a regular visitor to their home Strathallan Cliff where he and "Bob" Colby Cubbon were almost inseparable.

Many older Manx residents and visitors will remember the ***Glen Strathallan*** moored on the North Quay in the inner harbour at Douglas.

Following the Will, the ship was run by London County Council and her master was Capt. Glyn Griffiths. Sailing on the Thames and out into the Channel, Bruce carried on as Radio Officer, training cadets in the ***Glen Strathallan*** for years until the ship was finally taken out of service. As required under the Will, the ship was scuttled in Plymouth in about 1969. Bruce was 75 years of age when he left the sea finally and he really loved his little cabin right up in the fo'c'sle of the ***Glen Strathallan***.

The **Glen Strathallan** *in the River Thames.*
(photo: Authors collection)

The Contractors

Contract tickets, the Steam Packet name for season tickets, were normally issued for certain specific routes and periods. It was still possible to obtain an "All Stations" contractor's ticket permitting travel anywhere at any time but by 1983, these were becoming rare. For several years, when he was most journalistically active, the Company generously presented an

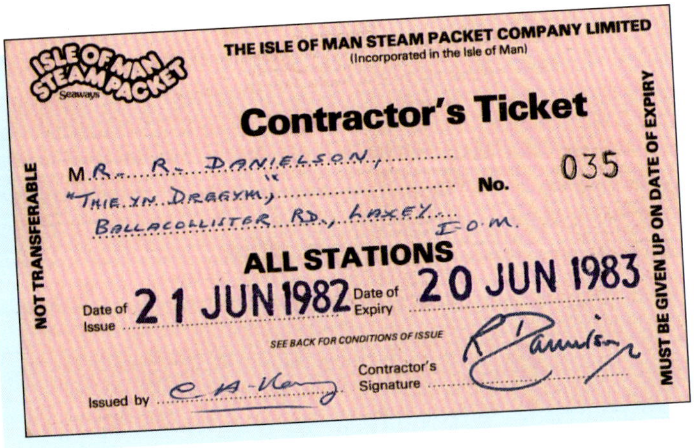

The author's 1982 "All Stations" Contract

"All Stations Contract" to the author thus facilitating the making of many interesting and some unscheduled voyages.

The holders of such tickets were called the "contractors" and were drawn in their hundreds to the old passenger boats and many remained faithful to the four car ferries thereafter. For no better reason than the pure pleasure of it and the good companionship it fostered, the "contractors" sailed back and forth in all weathers, all the year round. Immediately following the merger with Sealink early in 1985, the Liverpool service to the Isle of Man closed. It fell to the ***Mona's Queen*** and Capt. Bernard Quirk to sever the route amidst much emotion on 30th March 1985.

Sailing opportunities for Merseysiders had already been seriously diminished since 1982 with the cessation of the Llandudno service, but complete closure of the Liverpool route must have seemed to them, like the "last straw". Regular Liverpool-based voyages of the sort the "contractors" loved to make were thereby eliminated at a stroke, leaving them disenfranchised and believing that their patronage was no longer appreciated.

Although the Liverpool to Douglas service (L to D they called it, referring to the notation on the weekly typed sailing sheet) was later reinstated on a less frequent basis, it became rare to see the old personalities.

The author's good friend Ray Pugh was a very regular traveller as were his sister Barbara and her son Gordon Ditchfield. Well known book ship book publisher Leslie Stephenson and his wife Audrey would commute from Douglas to Liverpool weekly, and often more frequently, come rain or shine.

In their era most crossings would find several of the following aboard, always ready for a chat or just to pass a few pleasant hours in each others' company at sea:- Jerry Parkhill, Dolly Holland, Leslie Speller, Jim Robinson, Raymond Broderick, Jim Ford, Raymond Brandreth and his mother, Mr. Blackburn, Jerry Parkinson, Mary, Margaret and Jim Ford, Frank Thornley (author of the well known book on Liverpool & North Wales Steamers), Fred Henry (author of an earlier famous book about the Steam Packet and erstwhile resident of Laxey), Bill Flack, Tom Sargeant, Sid Savage, Jimmy Hornby, Ann Radcliffe, Eric Roughley (many of whose fine pencil drawings grace the collection of the author).

Barbara Ditchfield, Eddie Fox, Ray Pugh, Raymond Brandreth

Barbara and Gordon Ditchfield

Ray Pugh

Mrs. Holland

Messrs Hornby, Pugh, Robertson and Roughley (all photos: Ray Pugh)

George Boswell, George Bradshaw, Frank Pursal, Barry Roberts, Ken Foden, Mr. and Mrs. Savage, Mr. and Mrs. Dixon, John Milton, Mr. and Mrs. Pugh (no relation to Ray), Jimmy Hornby, Harold Ross, Ken Riding and John, Eddie Hall, Alan Duckett, John and Charles Marsh, Bill Bagshell, Ken Joplin, Reg Carson, Mr. and Mrs. Sharpe, Mrs and Miss Crellin, Dorothy Watnough, Rob Thompson, Mr. and Mrs. Savage, and countless more whose names now evade recollection.
For those whom the author has forgotten or never knew, let this be a tribute to all the "contractors".
No list of such seasoned travellers would be complete without mention of Mr Cecil Mitchell of Ballasalla, Isle of Man who, in recognition of his having made well over 4,500 crossings from the Island was recently made a "Freeman" of the Steam Packet Company enabling him to travel freely whenever he wishes.

Proud to be the Peveril

In this interesting, very early view of the ship as the **Holmia**, *she is thought to be at the fitting-out berth of her Norwegian shipbuilders.*

In 1973 a well known shipping giant, P. & O. chartered the ship for two years and ran her on the Heysham – Belfast service which they operated jointly with Sealink. P.& O. then bought the ship outright but after the service to Belfast ceased to be a joint one, they simply chartered the ship to Sealink. The ship was renamed **Penda** *in 1974 following the theme of "old monarch" names then popular. Here we see the ship as the* **Penda**, *arriving at Belfast in 1978 in the monastral blue colours of Sealink.*

In a whole page article in the Isle of Man Weekly Times dated 1st January 1985, the author published a long and detailed history of the***Peveril***, the first roll on – roll off vessel operated by the Steam Packet Company. In view of the announcement by Sea Containers' president, Jim Sherwood, that the existing fleet would be replaced in its entirety following his company's take over of the Steam Packet Company, news of which came on 29th March 1996, equity requires the book to salute the **Peveril** as well as its principal subjects, the four "side-loaders".

To quote from the author's Times article "*.....the* **Peveril** *has plodded her way back and forth with freight of all types keeping the wheels of Manx industry well oiled. So much so that readers will question whether it is possible to write an interesting piece about what, on the face of it, appears to be such a boring, unvarying subject*". In fact the article served to focus peoples' minds on the workhorse very well and for a long while thereafter, the **Peveril** was very much the centre of attraction in Douglas Harbour and the subject of many letters and telephone calls to the author.

Originally, she was built in 1971 at Kristiansand, Norway as the ***Holmia*** for Silja Line's Baltic Sea freight only service linking Sweden with Finland, calling at the Aland Islands also. She had a sistership, the ***Silvia***. Both were very well built and strengthened for working in ice too. Whilst neither had stabilisers, they were very sea kindly and Captain Peter Corrin and other masters all say that the ***Peveril*** is an excellent, strong ship and is safe in any storm. The ship was renamed ***ASD***

The **Holmia** *on night service in the Baltic port of Turku.*
Freighters tend to be scheduled to run overnight and round the clock. These days the **Peveril** *leaves Heysham in the middle of the night at 01.30, arriving at Douglas in time to commence unloading at 08.00. After two years as the* **Holmia**, *she was sold and became the* **ASD Meteor** *owned by International Ship Chartering Corporation of Singapore.*

Meteor in 1973, ***Penda*** in 1974 and ***NF Jaguar*** in 1980. Following the Steam Packet Company's decision to commence its own roll on – roll off freight service in 1981 the ***N F Jaguar*** was first taken on charter from P. & O. On 30th December 1982 James Fisher & Son Ltd. of Barrow-in-Furness purchased the ship from P. & O. (effectively on behalf of the Steam Packet Company) and she was demise chartered to the Manx Company in a financial arrangement at the end of which, the Steam Packet Company finally became the owners ten years later. How quickly we tend to forget that in those days, James Fisher & Son Ltd. were substantial shareholders in the Steam Packet Company, as indeed were the Isle of Man Government. The ***N F Jaguar*** was then formally renamed ***Peveril*** which name she adopted physically on 15th January 1983.

The **Peveril** *at Latchford Lock at midnight on 23rd/24th April 1983 during her voyage up the Manchester Ship Canal en route for United Ship Repairers yard by Mode Wheel Lock.*

In 1980, the ship had yet another change of name, this time she became the **N F Jaguar** *running the P. & O. freight service from Southampton to Le Harve in conjunction with the regular vessels* **Dragon** *and* **Leopard**. *N F were the initial letters of Normandy Ferries under which banner, that P. & O. route was marketed.*

(photos: Author / Author's collection)

The **Peveril** *as she looked when she emerged from her overhaul and complete repainting, at Manchester in 1983. Following his memorable voyage on the* **Peveril** *up the Manchester Ship Canal in April 1983, the author has come to hold the ship in great affection.*

After the merger between the Steam Packet Company and the Isle of Man services of Sealink/Manx Line in 1985 the ***Peveril*** became surplus to requirements. At that time the newly merged Steam Packet Company schedule provided two combined passenger and freight sailings a day to Heysham throughout the year, using the roll on-roll off multipurpose ships ***Mona's Isle*** and ***Manx Viking***.

The ***Peveril*** then went on charter to Belfast Freight Ferries Limited for service between Heysham and Belfast and later to Sealink, running from Stranraer to Larne. She returned to Steam Packet Company service at the end of 1986 and since then has been the very backbone of the freight side of the Company's business. The ***Peveril*** is the not only the oldest but the most profitable vessel in the fleet - and a fine ship she is too!

Coastwise Around the Island

The ships of the Isle of Man Steam Packet Company have been making trips around the coast of the Island since time immemorial. Some have been Round the Island, whilst others have been to view the Calf of Mann, to Port St. Mary and Port Erin and others have been to Ramsey and Peel. Peel has also been the destination for interesting trips organised by Tours Isle of Man, the coach operators and also some charters. Perhaps the most notable charter was when Captain Jack Ronan took a capacity crowd aboard the ***Mona's Queen*** from Heysham to Peel on what was Christened the Whalley Abbey Charter on 4th July 1987. For the benefit of his passengers, Captain Ronan virtually circumnavigated the Island, in glorious summer weather, arriving at Peel from the south and returning via Point of Ayre and Maughold.

The **Lady of Mann** *turns off Port St. Mary 28 May 1989.*

The **Mona's Queen** *alongside at Port St. Mary 30th June 1990.*

The **Mona's Queen** *arriving at Port St. Mary 30th June 1990.*

The **Lady of Mann** *passing Chicken Rock lighthouse 30th August 1987*

Left: The **Mona's Queen** *turns inside Port Erin Bay 30th June 1990.*

All the photographs are shown together in a medley starting at Douglas and sailing southabout right round the coast of the Island.

(all photos: Author)

Two photographs of the **Mona's Queen** *at Peel arriving on the Whalley Abbey Charter.*

Two photographs of the **Lady of Mann** *at Peel on 24th May 1992.*

The "Lady" crossing Laxey Bay returning to Douglas 19th May 1991.

The author's wife Pat and Capt. Tom Corteen 28th May 1989.

The **Lady of Mann** *at Ramsey 19th May 1991.*

Ships' Officers 1983

As with the previous lists of Officers, this list is compiled from the author's diaries, other records and was checked against official lists. The date chosen, 1983, could be described as the pinnacle of the car ferry era when all four were busily in service and at least two were operating all the year round.

In addition to the information they contain, reproduction of the lists is also intended to be a token of the author's appreciation of masters and officers, many of whom have been so generous in their help over the years. Some of these gentlemen are now, or have been, the superintendents, senior masters and officers of the company and to them and those who have retired also, the author offers a very hearty "thank you".

Masters and Mates 1983

Vessel	Master	Chief Officer	Second Officer
Lady of Mann	J.S. Kennaugh	R. Adams	T. Harrison
Mona's Queen	J.B. Quirk	S. Cowin	K. Buckle
Ben-my-Chree	J.E. Ronan	A. Bridson	J. Campbell
Manx Maid	E.C. Fargher	S. Hunter	A. Albitson
Relief	K. Bridson	C. Duggan	P. Shone
Relief	T.V. Kinley	D. Smith G. Peters	E. O'Toole
Peveril	P.C. Corrin D. Hall	N. Leece N. Wilde	M. Bregazzi N. Rainsford J. Kelly

Engineering Officers 1983

Vessel	Chief Engineer	2nd Engineer	3rd Engineer
Lady of Mann	A.F. Makin	W.N. Kelly	M. Livesey J. Clarke Electrician P. Thompson
Mona's Queen	M.C. Ramsay	J. Harper	K. Warrilow Electrician K. Roderick
Ben-my-Chree	P. MacAulay	R. Jones	J. Steel D. Pownall
Manx Maid	D.G. Minshall	R. Wales	W. Ahern C. Kneale
Peveril	W.R. Holmes M. Squibb	B. Trimble H. Crawley	D.J. Keggin D. Corlett J. Smyth
Relief Eng's	E.K. Convery B. Johnson D. Nelson	A. Lamberton K. Langdale B. Goldsmoth	W.H. Kermeen A. Warrilow A. Teare S. Moore W. Gelling I. McMurray

Success, Then Sad Decline

During those formative years of Manx Line and following its Fisher/Sealink take-over, travellers to the Island found themselves being conveyed on a seemingly never ending selection of quite delightful vessels which could themselves form the subject matter of another book. Such relief ships included the ***Viking III, Earl Godwin, Viking I, Antrim Princess,*** (which later became the ***Tynwald***) ***Ailsa Princess*** and the ***Villandry***. They were all roll on – roll off ships and their charters must have whetted the appetite of the Steam Packet Company directors. In the end the Steam Packet Company commenced its own roll on – roll off (freight only) service beginning in June 1981 using the P & O ferry ***N.F. Jaguar*** which was later renamed ***Peveril.*** For this they had constructed the second linkspan destined for Douglas Harbour.

Routine maintenance (and occasional breakdowns) of the rival **Manx Viking** *over the years brought about the introduction of various relief vessels on the Manx Line service. Here we see Thoresen Car Ferries* **Viking III, Viking 1** *in the Company of the* **Manx Maid** *and also the* **Lady of Mann** *with the French Sealink vessel* **Villandry.**

(photos: Author)

Right: Easter Monday, 12th April 1982 16.00. The **Lady of Mann** *awaits her trip to Dublin whilst the "Ben" is seen arriving from Liverpool. Following the fitting of their bow thrust units, the* **Ben-my-Chree** *and the* **Manx Maid** *were to be seen pumping copious volumes of water from the new bow thrust compartment forward.*
(photo: Author)

Below: The **Manxman** *has just arrived from Llandudno on 22nd July 1982 carrying plenty of passengers and is seen here berthing at the north side of the Victoria Pier where the* **Mona's Queen** *is already on the south side. The* **Mona's Queen** *was to take the afternoon Liverpool sailing at 16.00 whilst the* **Manxman** *had to return her day trip passengers to North Wales that evening prior to returning to Douglas.*
(photo: Author)

The ***Manxman*** survived until the end of 1982, the other old passenger steamers having previously been taken out of service, their fates sealed by the new rival ***Manx Viking.*** In truth, lovely old ships that they were, by then they were virtually obsolete. Their demise was as follows: the ***Snaefell*** in 1978, the ***Mona's Isle*** in 1980 and the ***Manxman*** two years later. The first two were sold for scrapping but the ***Manxman*** was sold for further static use in Preston, Liverpool and finally Hull, where she still remains.

In days gone by, the author quite often managed to make a quick exit from work in time to join the ***Manxman*** or one of her older sisters for the 18.00 return leg of the Llandudno day trip, sailing back to Douglas without passengers around midnight. The timetables were usually worked so that Llandudno sailings ran on two consecutive days causing the minimum of empty voyages to be necessary. On those occasions the ship would normally remain at Llandudno overnight either on the pier or anchored in the bay if wind was expected.

Right: The **Manxman** *berthed alongside and taking on oil for her bunkers from the* **Manx Maid** *on 16th August 1982. This low angle photograph was taken by the author from the Circus Beach beneath the old viaduct which has since been filled in and forms the new marshalling area between the two piers.*
(photo: Author)

Voyages undertaken at night always have a rather special quality. The ship is small and alone as she forges her way safely across the sea. One hears the sound of the waves but there is little to see in the darkness. Light from the windows and portholes reflects in the spray close by the ship. The "lume" from the navigation lights and smoke from the funnel all combine to capture a certain eeriness. Here we see the **Manx Maid** *at night on two occasions in 1981 and 1983 – but the dates are really irrelevant as the scenes are beautifully typical of them all. (photos: Author)*

The two steam powered car ferries could carry 1,400 passengers and the two motorships which were a little larger could carry 1,600. In this selection of photographs we amble gently all around the **Manx Maid** *and the* **Ben-my-Chree.** *How quickly we forget what it was like to travel on these delightful and practical ferries. Mary Masterton was one stewardess that the author came to know quite well, Paul the steward, also. They and their hardworking colleagues were excellent ambassadors for the Steam Packet Company. Whilst serving cups of coffee and tea, Bovril (yes, one really could have a cup of hot Bovril) pork pies, crisps and the like from their buffet hatch to the hundreds of people all wanting to be looked after instantly, they nearly always managed to look cheerful!*

One event that remains clearly in the author's mind was the sight of a young boy steward, seemingly no more than 16 year of age, who, complete with black bow tie and white shirt had fallen asleep on duty, in the middle of an overnight crossing on the "Ben" during the busy T.T. It was hard not to feel a lot of sympathy for that young man who clearly had been on his feet for far too long but, for his sin, was being berated by the Chief Steward.

Surprisingly, the ships escaped the worst of the graffiti artists endeavours, most of the time. One piece that the **Manx Maid** *took with her to the breakers yard was etched as deeply on one of her more private wooden doors as it was in the author's memory. It simply read "Life in .... is a sexually transmitted terminal disease." The name of the area has been deliberately omitted by the author for the sake of propriety - the comment could probably apply to a hundreds of problem inner city areas. The author apologises to those readers that this offends but in a book as much about the people as the ships, sad though the statement is, it begs inclusion. (photos: Author)*

When the **Mona's Queen** *came back on service for the 1983 season, she had been completely renovated including the fitting of new style seating, self service cafeteria, mother and baby room and new galleys. From the author's "Scene Afloat" series in the Isle of Man Weekly Times and elsewhere, dated 15th March 1983 (the 100th in the series) we read that £65,000 had been spent on the* **Mona's Queen** *in addition to the normal survey and overhaul costs. A video lounge and ship's shop were also promised. The new seats cost over £100 each and the pride and joy of the ship's cook was his new toaster capable of toasting 450 slices an hour!*
Taken during the course of the final few years of her service, here we see the ship having just arrived from Dublin with officers from H M Customs & Excise aboard, the shop created out of one of the former tea buffets, the baggage room and lower lounge. Mr J.A. (John) Humphrey, his present senior management title being Operations Manager, was respectively traffic and freight manager for years at about this time, and he succeeded such well know personalities as Mr. Eddie Lancaster and Alfie Maddrell in these roles. The author has always appreciated the kind words and helping hand freely given by John Humphrey on the occasions that it was clear such would be of assistance. *(photos: Author)*

On 23rd February 1983, a very rust streaked **Lady of Mann** *went off for overhaul having maintained the island lifeline throughout the winter.*
(photo: Author)

When the **Lady of Mann** *returned to service for the 1983 season on 31st March, she had been "adorned" with signwriting on her hull in the hope of attracting some free publicity when photographs of the Mersey were being shown on the television news etc. The signwriting proved to be almost unreadable, even at a short distance, and in the end it was replaced with far larger, clearer letters, but the whole concept was, to put it politely, not very subtle. The original version of the rubric is seen here in close-up at Douglas on the 31st March 1983, the day it was unveiled.* *(photo: Author)*

The **Lady of Mann** *had had a cafeteria fitted the previous year but for 1983, as can be seen from the photograph, her upper bar had been rebuilt as a magnificent Grill Room for which the first menu was as shown.*
(archive material and photo: Author)

The difficulty in reading the signwriting is obvious from this photograph of the ship as she sails up beautiful Belfast Lough on 16th July 1983 *(photo: Fred Rainey)*

This interesting scene dating from August 1983 is taken with the telephoto lens from the author's board room window in what is now Barclays Bank, looking down Victoria Street, Douglas. How quickly the scene has changed, the Villiers Hotel on the left is but a memory now! Captain Ronan was master and the **Ben-my-Chree** *is seen having just left the harbour and is commencing her sweep to get on course for Liverpool on the regular afternoon sailing.* *(photo: Author)*

By the time this classic photograph was taken showing the **Ben-my-Chree** *on senior race day, 10th June 1983, loading up for her 18.00 hrs sailing to Liverpool with Captain Ronan in command, she had been fitted with the triple chime steam whistle from the old passenger ship* **Tynwald.** *It is very low tide but to the flexible vehicle ramp system of the side-loading car ferries, this presented no problem. That day the author had made a round trip to Belfast with Captain Fargher, now commodore, aboard the* **Manx Maid** *returning shortly before the* **Ben-my-Chree** *departed. (photo: Author)*

Belfast

The **Manx Maid** *heads north to Belfast on T T Friday 10th June 1983. The steam turbine powered ships were wonderfully quiet in operation and on a warm day with a following breeze, there was nowhere better to sit, think and take in the view, than on the forward observation platform, looking out over the foc's'le. Listen carefully even now, and in one's imagination it might still be possible to hear the silky lapping of the sea, just as it was that calm summer's day as the ship's bow cut effortlessly through the water on her way to Ulster. If the tide was favourable, the journey took the ship north through Laxey Bay, past Maughold Head, Point of Ayre, Mull of Galloway, Copelands and on up through beautiful Belfast Lough with all its panoramic scenery. In the alternative, and surprisingly, there is little difference in the distance, the ship would sail south about. (photo: Author)*

The approach to Belfast aboard the **Manx Maid** *where the berth was at Pollock Basin at that time. (photo: Author)*

The **Manx Maid** *loading at Belfast's Pollock Dock in June 1983 and heading down the River Lagan leaving Belfast on her way back to the Isle of Man* *(photos: Author)*

The **Lady of Mann** *arrives at Belfast on 23rd May 1984.* *(photos: Author's collection)*

By May 1984, the wavy-line style of sign-writing tried on the ships in the previous year had given way to this bolder, but even more ugly script. Here we see both the **Lady of Mann** *and the* **Mona's Queen** *thus embellished (if that is the correct word).*
(photos: Author)

These photographs of the **Lady of Mann** *leaving Douglas were taken on 27th November 1984 in S.S.W. force 10 storm. The weather was so severe as to cause the ship to be on passage to Liverpool for almost six hours whilst her sister could not leave Liverpool until late afternoon when she experienced a very rough trip to the Island taking five and a half hours. Whilst on her sailing the previous night, the company's freighter,* **Peveril,** *had run for shelter off the Welsh coast where she hove-to until the storm moderated.*

(photos: Author)

The **Lady of Mann** *making a rather smokey departure from Fleetwood on 13th July 1981. Note how the dredged channel emerges near to the sandy foreshore outside the North Euston Hotel and sweeps to starboard almost immediately.*

On the next day, 14th July it was the **Manx Maid's** *turn to take the Fleetwood day trip and she is shown alongside. Even long after the old wooden berth had been condemned and replaced with a modern concrete one, the ships were always said to be alongside "the wharf" when at Fleetwood.*

(photos: Author)

A typical late September day, 1983 sees the commodore, Captain Kennaugh bring the **Lady of Mann** *in from Liverpool with passengers, cars and the Royal Mail. Note the mobile wooden booking office on the quayside from where one could buy a ticket, five minutes before departure! (photos: Author)*

The contract to carry the mail had been the very backbone of the Steam Packet existence since 1831 and was the principal reason for the year round service in both directions. Until 1974 the arrangements were with the British Post Office but following the creation of the Isle of Man Postal Authority and Manx postage stamps, the contract was thereafter agreed locally. These days, most mail is carried by aircraft.

Tynwald Day 1984. The **Manx Maid** *and the* **Lady of Mann** *are seen at Douglas, dressed overall for the occasion.*

(photos: Author)

After long periods of discussion and consultation throughout the late 1970s and early 1980s on the subject of roll on – roll off operations, towards the end of October 1984 the Steam Packet Company bought from Maltese owners, the former Townsend Thoresen Car Ferries ship, **Free Enterprise III.** *She went to the Clyde for major works to enable her to carry more freight and cars.*
The ship was renamed **Mona's Isle** *but in windy conditions, she was impossible to handle and could not berth unaided. She is seen here on 21st April 1985, beam on to the end of the Victoria Pier, whilst a decision was made as to how and where she might be berthed.*
(photo: Author)

The **Mona's Isle** *dominates the Douglas Harbour skyline – with all that top hamper and an underpowered bowthruster, it is hardly surprising that she was susceptible to even the slightest wind.* *(photo: Author)*

On 1st February 1985 the Island was stunned by publication of the news that the Isle of Man Steam Packet Company had merged with the Manx shipping operations of Sealink U.K. In future, all year services would be to the Sealink Port of Heysham, not Liverpool, and would be maintained by the newly purchased ship renamed ***Mona's Isle*** and a chartered Sealink vessel. In the event the ***Mona's Isle*** was not a success and was sold to Saudi Arabian interests after the 1985 season. To be a good marketing executive which he was, takes a special breed of person who is eternally optimistic and not easily daunted by even the worst shocks. The author recalls a telephone conversation with Mr. R.L. (Dick) Reeves in which the stoical marketing man advised him that the Steam Packet Company had just taken over Sealink! Dick was a good and loyal friend throughout and always found time to help the author.

(archive material: Author's collection)

ISLE OF MAN STEAM PACKET
Seaways
P.O. Box 5, DOUGLAS.
Tel. 0624–23344 Telex 629414

1st February, 1985.

TO TRAVEL AGENTS AND TOUR OPERATORS

Dear Customer,

ISLE OF MAN PASSENGER AND COMMERCIAL SEA SERVICES

In early April 1985 the sea transport services currently operated to the Isle of Man from England by the Steam Packet Company and Sealink British Ferries will be integrated and operations moved to the port of Heysham. **Isle of Man sailings from Liverpool will then be discontinued.**

The Steam Packet multi-purpose Ro-Ro vessel MONA'S ISLE will be joined by the ANTRIM PRINCESS, on charter from Sealink British Ferries, to maintain an all the year round passenger and full load freight Ro-Ro service between Heysham and the Isle of Man. The shorter sea route will effect a saving in sailing time and operating costs, and will not only safeguard the continuation of adequate passenger and freight services to the Isle of Man, but also improve them.

The seasonal services to Ardrossan, Belfast, Dublin and Fleetwood will continue to be operated by the car ferries LADY OF MANN and MONA'S QUEEN.

We enclose our "advance information" leaflet. The new Steam Packet sailing brochures covering all routes will be delivered to you in about two weeks.

Assuring you of our best attention at all times.

Yours faithfully,

Dick Reeves

Marketing Executive.

CARRIAGE OF PASSENGERS AND THEIR ACCOMPANIED LUGGAGE, VEHICLES AND DOMESTIC ANIVALS IS SUBJECT TO THE COMPANY'S STANDARD CONDITIONS OF CARRIAGE OF PASSENGERS AND PASSENGERS' ACCOMPANIED PROPERTY, WHICH INCORPORATE THE PROVISIONS OF THE ATHENS CONVENTION, 1974. ALL OTHER CARRIAGE IS SUBJECT TO THE COMPANY'S STANDARD CONDITIONS OF CARRIAGE OF GOODS. COPIES OF BOTH SETS OF CONDITIONS ARE AVAILABLE ON APPLICATION TO ANY OF THE COMPANY'S OFFICES

The author's photograph of the **Manx Maid** *took pride of place on the front cover of the Christmas edition of the well known international shipping magazine Sea Breezes and was a good advertisement for the Isle of Man. Here we see the well laden* **Manx Maid** *turning in Douglas harbour with the aid of her bowthruster on her afternoon departure to Fleetwood on August Bank Holiday 1984.* *(photo: Author)*

Sadly, at the end of the 1984 summer season, the two oldest car ferries, the steam powered ***Manx Maid*** and the ***Ben-my-Chree,*** were simultaneously withdrawn as there was no longer business for them and the Company had just taken the decision to operate a roll on – roll off multipurpose ship in addition to the ro – ro freighter ***Peveril,*** introduced three years earlier. In fact, even though the ***Ben-my-Chree*** was then sold and was expected to cross the Atlantic for static work in Jacksonville, America, she became registered in Liverpool and the following year was chartered back by the Steam Packet Company to help out with the peak T.T. traffic of 1985.

Right: The **Ben-my-Chree's** *charter was on a reduced passenger certificate for 750 passengers for the two busy weeks of T.T. 1985. She operated between Heysham and Douglas and as fate would have it, these were the only occasions in her whole career when she visited Heysham. Capt. D.C. (David) Hall took the ship into and out of Heysham for the first time ever on 25th May 1985. Engineer Willy Gelling, Dave Pownall and colleagues wrestled with the task of keeping the ship running, although she had had virtually no maintenance since being taken out of service the previous year. The author made the first trip out of Heysham aboard the unkempt "Ben" and it was sad to see how quickly she had deteriorated since being sold by the Steam Packet Company.* *(photos: Author)*

The **Manx Maid** *at Avonmouth photographed on 24th August 1985.*
(photo: Author)

DEPARTMENT OF ~~TRADE~~ TRANSPORT
Marine Survey Office
221 Graeme House Derby Square Liverpool L2 7SQ
Telex 628474 Answer Back DOT LVG
Telephone 051-236 6901

Please reply to the Principal Officer
Your reference

The Tug Master

Our reference

Date 1st April 198

Dear Sir~~s~~

m.v. "MANX MAID"
LOAD LINE EXEMPTION CERTIFICATE
FAVOURABLE WEATHER CONDITIONS

You will note on the attached certificate that one of the conditions for the exemption of the ship from the stated sections of the Act and of the Rule requirements is that the ship should operate only when weather conditions and official weather forecasts for the period of the voyage are favourable. This is a compensatory measure to offset the failure to reach full compliance with the statutory requirements. Although there is no legal definition of these conditions it is intended that they should be interpreted by the ship's Master as being:-

> "Weather, when the visibility is good, and when the combined effects of wind, sea or swell, upon the ship under consideration are never greater than those which would cause moderate rolling or pitching, or result in the shipping of green seas on to the weather deck."

It will of course be appreciated that the above interpretation could vary considerably according to the size, type and sea handling capabilities of the ship under consideration, the force, direction, fetch and duration of the wind and also with the intended area of operation. Consequently a sound working knowledge of the ship and its behaviour under varying weather conditions, the area of operation, plus careful and regular attention to official weather forecasts is all important.

Yours faithfully

M Foot.

The ***Manx Maid*** was sold in early 1985 and on 10th April was towed to Avonmouth for the start of her expected new life in retirement moored in Bristol's City docks. She had gone into dry-dock prior to the tow to have her stabilisers removed for future use on the ***Mona's Isle*** that had ineffective water filled "Flume" tank stabilisers. The problems with the ***Mona's Isle*** mentioned earlier meant that they were never fitted and in the author's opinion it is doubtful whether they would have been effective on a ship with so much larger dimensions anyway.

The author has the original letter dated 1st April 1985 from the Department of Transport to the master of the tug ***Wallasey***, that was to tow the ***Manx Maid*** to Avonmouth. The care and attention to detail for the voyage was quite intense.

(archive material: Authors Collection)

Ardrossan

Three views of the **Ben-my-Chree** *heading for Ardrossan. The first two were taken on 3rd July 1982 from the bridge of the* **Manxman** *on her last ever voyage from Ardrossan. The author and Douglas lightkeeper Alistair Henderson had made the voyage north the night before. Captain Hall was in the* **Manxman** *and Captain Ronan was in the "Ben". As the two ships came into range, Captain Ronan called up the* **Manxman** *on the V.H.F. radio to ask if he might come a little closer as a number of his passengers had made the trip especially to be able to see the* **Manxman.** *As the two ships closed to safe navigation distance at a combined speed of 42 knots, there was much cheering and waving. Plenty of steam was used as the ships exchanged noisy salutes in the traditional way.*
The final photograph is included to show the comparison with the bold hull rubric applied in 1984. *(photos: Author)*

Right: The Ardrossan route was one casualty of the merger with Sealink but in truth, traffic had been poor for many seasons prior to 1985 when the **Mona's Queen** *finally closed the route on 25th August. There followed a short-lived service to Stranraer which was no more successful than that to its more northern predecessor. Previously, on 30th March 1985, with Captain J.B. (Bernard) Quirk in command, the* **Mona's Queen** *closed down the Liverpool route and likewise Fleetwood at the end of the season also as a direct result of the merger. Thankfully, both of these routes have since been reinstated.* *(photo: David Parsons)*

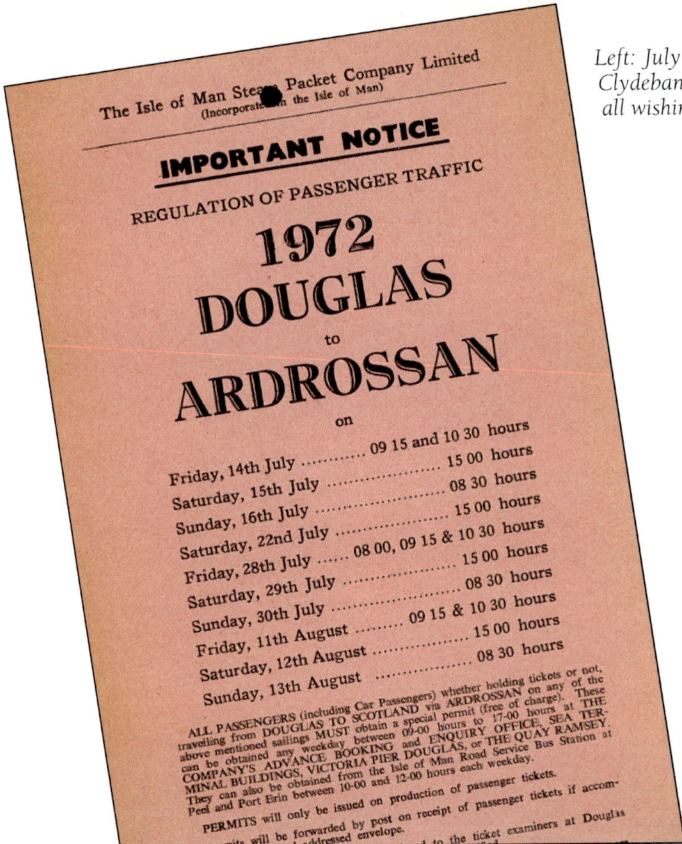

The Isle of Man Steam Packet Company Limited
(Incorporated in the Isle of Man)

IMPORTANT NOTICE

REGULATION OF PASSENGER TRAFFIC

1972
DOUGLAS
to
ARDROSSAN
on

Friday, 14th July .... 09 15 and 10 30 hours
Saturday, 15th July .... 15 00 hours
Sunday, 16th July .... 08 30 hours
Saturday, 22nd July .... 15 00 hours
Friday, 28th July ...... 08 00, 09 15 & 10 30 hours
Saturday, 29th July .... 15 00 hours
Sunday, 30th July .... 08 30 hours
Friday, 11th August .... 09 15 & 10 30 hours
Saturday, 12th August .... 15 00 hours
Sunday, 13th August .... 08 30 hours

ALL PASSENGERS (including Car Passengers) whether holding tickets or not, travelling from DOUGLAS TO SCOTLAND via ARDROSSAN on any of the above mentioned sailings MUST obtain a special permit (free of charge). These can be obtained any weekday between 09-00 hours to 17-00 hours at THE COMPANY'S ADVANCE BOOKING and ENQUIRY OFFICE, SEA TERMINAL BUILDINGS, VICTORIA PIER DOUGLAS, or THE QUAY RAMSEY. They can also be obtained from the Isle of Man Road Service Bus Station at Peel and Port Erin between 10-00 and 12-00 hours each weekday.

PERMITS will only be issued on production of passenger tickets.

Permits will be forwarded by post on receipt of passenger tickets if accompanied by a stamped addressed envelope.

Left: July 1972 handbill for peak sailings in respect of the Scottish holidays. Glasgow, Clydebank, Greenock, Edinburgh and Aberdeen all produced thousands of holiday makers, all wishing to get away and back during the months of July and August.
(archive material: Author)

Above: The **Lady of Mann** *seen crossing Laxey Bay heading north to Ardrossan. Ardrossan harbour was home for many years to Burns & Laird Line and their service to Belfast, and actively continues thus for the Caledonian MacBrayne Limited service to Brodick on the Isle of Arran. For over ninety years from about 1890, except in wartime, the Steam Packet Company used Ardrossan as it summer destination for Scottish passengers. It was and remains a difficult harbour to enter during gales as it is very exposed. These days a very limited service is operated on summer weekends only to the Isle of Man.* *(photo: Author)*

Here we see the **Mona's Queen** *on 16th July 1983, Glasgow Fair Saturday, with a small crowd gathered to welcome her alongside at the Winton Pier.*
(photo: Author's collection)

The **Lady of Mann** *and by way of design comparison, the Arran ferry* **Isle of Arran** *(belonging to Caledonian MacBrayne) in June 1985.*
(photo: Author)

Manx Maid – Rest in Peace

The **Manx Maid** *was broken up at Garston in the Spring of 1986. Clearly the old ship's days are over and in this series of photographs taken over a period of about two months the ship disappears before our eyes.*

(photos: Gordon Ditchfield)

Sadly, planning approval for the ***Manx Maid*** venture was not forthcoming and after languishing at Avonmouth for ten months or so, the following February she was towed back to the Mersey where she was broken up at Garston, opposite her original birthplace.
Through the good offices of his friend Derek Medlock, the author was able to add to his collection of ships' brasses and other memorabilia when the ***Manx Maid*** was being broken up. This was no mean feat for Derek as he is a powerfully built fellow and to access the ship, he had to scramble across a rather frail wooden ladder lying horizontally between shore and ship which were several feet apart! Notwithstanding, a price for some excellent pieces was negotiated with the scrapyard and after much hard labour, Derek retrieved them and they now are polished regularly by the author's wife!
Amongst the articles saved and now in the author's collection is the ship's last bridge log book which was still in the drawer in the captain's desk in his cabin, just as it was on the day it was last written up when Capt. Vernon Kinley took her from Douglas to Liverpool for the last time on 10th September 1984. Marine Superintendent Capt. Harvey Collister authorised the final entry in the log "Ships Articles closed on 11th September 1984" adding a certain finality to the sad proceedings.

This photograph of the entire Steam Packet fleet was one of a series that the author took on the morning of Tynwald Day 1987 and which were used on the front cover of the Steam Packet Company Annual Report and Accounts 1987 and also on the front pages of the local newspapers at a time when colour was in its infancy on locally published newsprint. *(photo: Author)*

Following the merger with Sealink the Fleetwood service ended. However, in conjunction with Associated British Ports (owners of Fleetwood Harbour) a series of trips were operated under the banner of "The Funboat". Here we see the **Mona's Queen** *at Douglas, slumbering in the afternoon sunshine, before making ready for Captain Kinley to take her on the return leg of the first "Funboat" from Fleetwood on 1st July 1986.*

(photo: Author, archive material: Author's collection)

Above: On 31st March 1988 the ferry/cruise ship **Norrona** *visited Douglas on a cruise. She is seen here with the* **Mona's Queen** *which has just arrived from Liverpool and will shortly re-load and sail to Dublin for one of several Easter trips.*

(photo: Author)

Below: In April 1988, the **Mona's Queen** *had an interesting charter to Sealink when she operated their renowned Holyhead-Dun Laoghaire service for two weeks. She is seen here early in the morning on the first day of the service at Dun Laoghaire.*

(photo: Russell Plummer, ferry correspondent, Ships Monthly)

In April 1988 the regular Holyhead mailboat, ***St. Columba,*** was off service having her overhaul and her relief, the ***St. David***, had had a fire on board and was therefore out of action. As a result Sealink were in real trouble.

However, duly chartered, the combined capacity of the Steam Packet Company's ***Mona's Queen*** and the ***Peveril*** carrying freight at weekends, saved the day. The alternative would have been for the ***Mona's Queen*** to go to Dover to run the Golden Arrow service and for a Dover ship to come round to Holyhead. The prospect of such a relatively small ship doing such a big job so valiantly was reminiscent of David and Goliath !

Dublin

The Tynwald Day excursion to Dublin on 5th July 1989 will be one remembered for many years to come. Of hundreds of day cruises made by the author, it ranks high amongst the best. In glorious weather, Captain Vernon Kinley took what seemed like half the population of the Island on this trip aboard the **Mona's Queen.** *The sun was really hot and with a following breeze, the car ramps quickly became a haven for sun bathers. In these three photographs, we see the* **Mona's Queen** *sailing south with her passengers spread out on the car ramps, taking the Dublin Pilot on board and finally, we see the ship berthed in the River Liffey in Dublin, at her berth near the city centre. (photos: Author)*

The ***Ben-my-Chree****, having failed to find a buyer after being finally withdrawn from service following her charter back to the Steam Packet Company for the 1985 T.T., was towed away to Santander on August 16th 1989 and arrived at the north Spanish port where she is seen in this photograph five days later, where she was to be broken up.*

(photo: Author's collection)

Following her rebuilding, the **Lady of Mann** *had an even greater capacity for carrying vehicles and in T.T. week has been known to regularly carry over 350 motor-cycles or more than 130 cars per voyage.* *(photo: Author)*

Even though the car ferries carried only little over half the numbers of say, the old ***Lady of Mann,*** by the late 1980s there was almost no call for the ability to carry more than 1,000 passengers at a time. However, vehicle numbers were on the increase relative to overall passenger figures and it became necessary to find a way of increasing vehicle capacity significantly.

At the beginning of January 1989, the Steam Packet Company contracted with Wright & Beyer Ltd. of Birkenhead in a sum exceeding £2,500,000 for the virtual rebuilding of the ***Lady of Mann.*** The ship was literally gutted and for a time was held together (or apart to be more precise) with the maritime equivalent of "Accro" props. Gone was all her internal accommodation, bar, cabins, lounges, cafeteria and everything became open plan.

Decks became identified with letters. "A" Deck, being the upper boat deck onto which new passenger cabins would be built, was covered with teak planking, having previously been bare steel. "B" Deck encompassed the main lounges, shop, toilets, information desk and cafe. "C" Deck was dramatically transformed with a new lower lounge into which a complete new row of forward facing windows were built looking straight out at the foc's'le. Abaft the lounge were toilets and a new bar (which had no windows at all) and further aft still was the new upper car deck that could carry forty or fifty small cars. This transformed the vehicle carrying capacity of the vessel and she can now carry over 130 vehicles.

Unfortunately the work on the ship was late being completed and she emerged with a temporary passenger certificate for 950 to enable T.T. traffic to be carried prior to the work being finished. Her livery was changed and whilst in itself it was attractive, the alterations to the ship which had copious windows plated over or blanked off had rather detracted from her previous good looks. The results of the conversion were excellent and the ship became an equal partner in the fleet once again instead of being the hybrid she had become, following the roll on – roll off revolution and the merger.

It had been planned to send the ship on a series of goodwill cruises to Londonderry, Dublin and Belfast but these and trips round the Island coast to Peel were cancelled when the ship was not ready in time. Here the author would like to place on record his thanks and congratulations to the present management of the Company who have been willing to operate some interesting trips of recent years and perhaps will do so again in 1996?

Is it too much to hope that, in otherwise idle moments scheduled for Liverpool on Wednesday afternoons in September 1996, the "Lady" may make a nostalgic excursion to Llandudno?

Right: The need for the passenger ships to be able to carry such large numbers of passengers was no longer paramount and it was only in the busy T.T. period that capacities were like to be severely tested. This photograph is of the **Lady of Mann** *loading for a June 1984 departure with T.T. traffic returning from Douglas.*

(photo: Author)

Above: The finished article. This photograph of the **Lady of Mann** *in her fine new livery was used by the author on the front cover of the book, The Very Best of British Book 1. The book sold thousands of copies and in the process, promoted the Steam Packet Company internationally.*

(photo: Author)

Right: In this photograph, the **Lady of Mann** *has just been rebuilt and is in the process of receiving her new livery on 30th April 1989.*

(photo: Gordon Ditchfield)

The **Lady of Mann** *arriving at Douglas on 7th March 1996.*
(photo: Author)

RECOMMISSIONING
OF THE
LADY OF MANN

The Chairman, Mr N R Corlett, and Directors of the Isle of Man Steam Packet Company request the pleasure of the company of
Mr and Mrs R G Danielson
at the recommissioning of the M V LADY OF MANN, which will take place in Douglas Harbour on Friday 19 May 1989.

12.00 Reception on Board

12.30 Recommissioning of vessel by Mrs N R Corlett

13.00 Buffet lunch

RSVP
Mrs M King
Imperial Buildings
Douglas
Isle of Man

The **Lady of Mann's** *recommissioning ceremony and celebration cruise was deferred a week or so to permit the works to be completed. The ceremony was performed by Mrs. Corlett, wife of the Chairman, Norman Corlett on the afternoon of 28th May 1989.*

Tickets for the deferred celebration cruise were not reprinted and were used on the evening of 28th May 1989, when the trip was finally run. On this trip and on many other outings, the author and his wife Pat accompanied their good friend, retired Captain Tom Corteen.
(archive material: Author's collection)

Having closed the Stranraer service a few days earlier, the ***Mona's Queen*** then had another interesting job to do. She left Fleetwood on 31st August 1989 bound for Cherbourg where she was to pick up 1,000 spectators (and thence to Portsmouth to uplift a few more) who were there supporting the French Post Office entry ***La Poste*** at the start of the Round the World Yacht race. Following the ***La Poste*** charter, she immediately went on service for Sealink covering their Cherbourg, Portsmouth and Guernsey route for the damaged ***Earl Granville*** and then went on to Weymouth to cover for the ***Earl Godwin.*** She finally completed these duties on 23rd September 1989 and sailed back to Douglas to unload her car ramps, prior to going into dock for the winter.

The **Mona's Queen** *was scheduled to arrive back in the Isle of Man at 07.45 on 25th September 1989 after her long sail up from Weymouth. Almost to the second, Captain Kinley brought the ship alongside the Victoria Pier in the presence of the then entire fleet. It proved to be the last such occasion for the* **Mona's Queen, Lady of Mann, Tynwald** *(ex* **Antrim Princess**) *and* **Peveril.** *(photos: Author)*

The **Mona's Queen** *at Portsmouth on 2nd September 1989.*
(photo: David Parsons)

1990 turned out to be the final season in service for the **Mona's Queen.** *Before she retired at the end of the season she operated a coastal cruise landing at Port St. Mary on 30th June in celebration of the Company's 160th Anniversary. On 24th July 1990 she was called upon to carry out yet another interesting task.*

This was in connection with the 150th Anniversary of the Cunard Line and for this the famous liner **Queen Elizabeth 2** *was to visit the Mersey for the very first time. Under Captain Kinley, himself a time served Cunard man, the* **Mona's Queen** *made a specially retimed excursion to Liverpool where she enjoyed an historic meeting with the* **Queen Elizabeth 2.** *When the Manx ship departed from the Landing Stage at Liverpool on her return trip to Douglas, she sailed right round the mighty liner which was anchored midstream, both ships exchanging throaty blasts on their sirens. The author had been the guest of Mersey Ferries for the day and from his vantage point on the bridge of the ferry* **Overchurch**, *which was acting as tender for the liner, he was able to cover every aspect of the proceedings. The main photograph and a long article by the author appeared in Sea Watch (the Steam Packet Company's house magazine), other national shipping journals and a very similar view was the subject of a new Manx postage stamp.*
(photo. Author)

ISLE OF MAN POST OFFICE AUTHORITY

£1 ISLE OF MAN

HIGH VALUE SHIPS DEFINITIVE STAMPS

The Chairman, Members and Director of the Isle of Man Post Office Authority cordially invite you to a presentation to mark the issue of their High Value Ships Definitive Stamps

on board the King Orry, Victoria Pier, Douglas Harbour on Wednesday September 15th 1993

from 10.30 am to 12 noon only.

RSVP to: Post Office: 686103

Wine / Fruit juice
Commemorative Items

The ***Mona's Queen*** ended her 1990 sailing season in uncharacteristic disarray. The normally utterly reliable, now eighteen years old, first diesel powered passenger ship in the Manx Fleet was outward bound from Liverpool on the evening of Sunday, 2nd September on what was to have been her last Liverpool round trip before laying up. Half an hour out, the intercooler between turbo blower and the starboard engine failed allowing sea water to enter the cylinders of the main engines. She managed to limp to Douglas on just her port engine where she arrived over 6 hours later. Next day she returned to Liverpool carrying cars only whilst her passengers went to Heysham on the newly acquired ***Channel Entente*** (later renamed ***King Orry***). The ***Mona's Queen*** was then laid up and offered for sale as the combined car carrying capacity of the rebuilt ***Lady of Mann*** and the ***King Orry*** would in future be sufficient.

The **Mona's Queen,** *departing from Liverpool Landing Stage, sets off to sail round the* **Queen Elizabeth 2** *anchored in the Mersey.*
(photo : John Collins)

Seen here in royal company, the **Lady of Mann** *and the* **Mona's Queen** *with H M Yacht* **Britannia** *and her naval escort in the background photographed on 8th August 1989.* *(photos: Author)*

Liverpool Scenes

Above and Below: The **Ben-my-Chree** *berthing alongside Liverpool Landing stage on 16th February 1982. (photos: Gordon Ditchfield)*

21st December 1990 saw the ***Lady of Mann*** hurriedly brought out of dock for a charter to B & I Line on their Holyhead – Dublin route. Working two round trips a day, the ***Lady of Mann*** was responsible for carrying a very large proportion of the Irish population going home for Christmas that year.

No sooner had the ***Lady of Mann*** returned to her slumbers than she was out again relieving the ***St. Columba*** again on the Holyhead – Dun Laoghaire service, but this time for Sealink. During this stint she encountered some very bad weather resulting in her Sealink masters and officers bestowing the nick name *"The Submarine"* upon her. Apparently, so the story goes, they were so used to the lofty heights of the bridge of their normal ship, the large ***St. Columba,*** that when they took over the ***Lady of Mann*** and ventured out in their first storm, they found themselves uncomfortably close to the sea (when not actually watching the bows diving under it). In the beginning, this was a very new experience for them and as a result she earned herself the affectionate nick name! By all accounts, the "Lady" served them well and maintained the service efficiently.

Above: September 1984, and the **Manx Maid**, *shown to advantage against the famous Liverpool waterfront, was by then about to be withdrawn from service. (photo: Author)*

Left: The **Lady of Mann** *alongside the Liverpool Landing Stage on 14th April 1990. (photo: Author)*

The ***Lady of Mann*** undocked from Birkenhead on 25th May 1993, marking the beginning of her season with a very special duty. At 07.00 on 26th May 1993 with Captain Fargher in command, the ***Lady of Mann*** took 492 passengers from Liverpool in gale force conditions to represent the merchant service in the Battle of the Atlantic celebrations off Anglesey. The ship rode out the gale for eight hours in the company of the H.M. Yacht ***Britannia*** and a large contingent of naval ships.

At the same time, the excursion ship ***Balmoral*** had paid an historic first visit to Morecambe from where she sailed with the author on board, via Blackpool to Merseyside, ready to join up with the ***Lady of Mann*** off Anglesey. Although she reached Liverpool safely, sadly, conditions were too rough for the ***Balmoral*** to join the ***Lady of Mann*** in the cavalcade.

Four days later on 30th May the ***Lady of Mann*** took a cruise to Port St. Mary thereby following in the wake of her older sister the ***Mona's Queen***, that had made the trip three years previously.

Above: A tranquil scene at Douglas showing the **Balmoral** *and the* **Peveril** *at 07.30 on 14th June 1989.*

Below: Another early morning scene, this time showing the **Balmoral** *in her new livery with the* **Lady of Mann** *in the background at 07.30 on 25th June 1993.*

(photos: Author)

Misfortune struck the **Lady of Mann** *on her sailing from Liverpool on 2nd June 1993. Through what was later described as a "misunderstanding", upon her arrival at Douglas the ship collided with the Battery Pier causing herself very considerable damage. This was right in the middle of the busy T.T. period and the Company had to make hasty arrangements with other operators to cover the next few days sailings.* **Seacat Scotland** *and Caledonian MacBrayne's ferry* **Pioneer** *were called upon to help out. Meanwhile, the* **Lady of Mann** *was inspected by the Isle of Man Government Marine Administration and a new collision bulkhead was constructed abaft the ships shattered bow. Still bruised and battered the ship returned to service but following the T.T. she was able to be withdrawn for permanent repairs.*

This excellent press photograph was taken by Brian Mitchell, a local professional photographer. Brian is not only an excellent photographer but also a well known and accomplished musician.

(photo: Brian Mitchell)

Near riot waiting for delayed ferry

SIR — While in the Isle of Man for the TT, I chanced to see an item in your paper on the subject of the unfortunate accident which befell the Lady of Mann.

The impression given by your article seemed to imply that passengers were subject to a slight inconvenience as a result but that the Steam Packet Company had quickly and efficiently got matters under control and passengers had been subjected to delays of less than 12 hours.

Nothing could be further from the truth. My companions and I

his motorcycle, only a passenger ticket, yet because he was standing next to a motorcycle he was issued with a boarding card for his machine!

Another individual claimed to have obtained a boarding pass for £100. This individual arrived 30 minutes before we were allowed on to the landing stage immediately prior to boarding and pushed his machine to the front of the melee and boarded the ship before those of us who had sp... most of the day on the d...

3. There was n...

FRIDAY, 25th JUNE, 1993 No. 696

'MISUNDERSTANDING' CAUSED FERRY CRASH

Whilst the ship was lucky to escape her ordeal, the Steam Packet Company came in for some fairly harsh criticism from inconvenienced passengers, the worst of whose understandable acerbity was reproduced for all to see in the local press for several editions following the incident.

(archive material: Authors collection)

On 4th June 1994 and not for the first time, the Polish sail training ship, **Dar Mlodziezy**, *visited the Isle of Man. Captain Vernon Kinley in the* **Lady of Mann** *took the opportunity to sail right round the visitor, thus affording his passengers an excellent view. In accordance with maritime custom, both ships dipped their ensigns as a mark of recognition and respect. The author recalls that when the Manx lighthouses were manned (they have since been mostly automated) ensigns on the lighthouse yard-arm and on the ship were often dipped as ships passed. Occasionally, this happened unexpectedly but in true tradition, and never to be seen to be discourteous, the author has been privileged to witness the Chief Officer, literally running to the stern of the ship to dip the ensign after hearing the master calling to him "She's dipping"! In the good old days when the cost of a gallon of diesel fuel to run the compressors was not so great, the lighthouse fog horn might also be sounded as the ship sped past and what an unmistakably mournful bellowing sound it was too, quite unlike the electronic "ping" of today's fog warnings. (photos: Author)*

The ***Seacat Isle of Man*** on trials 23rd June 1994, with the (former train ferry) ***King Orry*** in the background.
(photo: Author)

Board of Directors 1960 to April 1996

The Isle of Man Steam Packet Company Limited

M.P. Aiken	1991	– 1994
A. Alexander	<1960	– 1985
D.G. Benson	1994	– current board member
T.E. Brownsdon	1965	– 1983
E.C.B. Corlett	1981	– 1985
N.R. Corlett	1984	– 1992
W.E. Costain	1964	– 1972
K.C. Cowley	1969	– 1983
J.F. Crellin	<1960	– 1970
P.G. Crellin	1985	– current board member
D. Dixon	1986	– current Managing Director*
J.B. Garside	<1960	– 1975
W.A. Gilbey	1975	– current board member
B.A. Holt	1983	– 1984
J.H. Kelly	1992	– current Chairman
W.C. Kelly	1963	– 1969
F.C. Kissack	1971	– 1981
A.E. Kitto	<1960	– 1965
N.B. Martin	1992	– current Finance Director*
L.C. Merryweather	1985	– 1985
W.M. Musgrave-Hoyle	<1960	– 1971
J.R. Quayle	<1960	– 1963
J.E.K. Rae	1971	– 1985
H.A.C. Ross	1992	– current board member
J.B. Sherwood	1985	– current board member
S.R. Shimmin	1972	– 1985
R.T.D. Stott	1984	– current board member
M.J.L. Stracey	1985	– 1986
R.M. Synge	<1960	– 1964
N.J. Tatham	1985	– 1991

*These two directors are expected to resign following the Sea Containers' take-over bid announced on 29th March 1996.

Above: This is a classic study of the Steam Packet Company board of directors in formal pose in 1975 with the builder's model of the **Mona's Queen.** *Major Brownsdon was appointed Chairman in succession to Mr J.B. Garside when he relinquished the position (but remained a director) in 1972 after 20 years excellent service to the company.*
Major Brownsdon went on to serve the Company in exemplary manner as director and Chairman of the Board for a further eleven years.
Back row (left to right): W.A. Gilbey, F.C. Kissack, J.E.K. Rae and S.R. Shimmin.
Front row (left to right): A. Alexander (Deputy Chairman) T.E. Brownsdon (Chairman) and K.C. Cowley.

Right: The "old school".
At the end of 1982, whilst remaining a director and then becoming Chairman of the Board, Mr Sydney Shimmin (centre) retired as general manager of the Steam Packet Company in favour of his assistant Mr Ronnie Kissack (left). Mr Eric Cretney (right) became the new assistant manager prior to his elevation to the top job when Mr Kissack retired two years later. The author wishes to place on record his appreciation for all the help and recognition these three gentlemen gave to him during their long periods of office in their respective duties.

End of the Era

Following the introduction of the fast craft ***Seacat Isle of Man*** in June 1994, the ***Lady of Mann*** saw no Manx service other than as relief ship covering the ***King Orry's*** overhaul in February and early March 1995 and as additional tonnage to assist with the 1995 Manx T.T. motorcycle race traffic.

In fact, many feared that when Captain Vernon Kinley sailed the "Lady" away from Douglas on 28th June 1994 witnessed by the author, Steam Packet Company supporter Jean Evans, and a very small handful of others, she might never be seen again. These fears were very real despite talk of finding other work for her. *A medley of photographs of the event appears on page 120.* A service from Fleetwood/ Blackpool to Dublin was one option considered as was Liverpool to Belfast and a service across the North Sea to the Continent. Whilst the Steam Packet Company is to be commended for its efforts to keep the ship in service and her men in full employment, no new domestic service materialised.

However, after a short lay up in Birkenhead, on 17th July 1995, the ***Lady of Mann*** left Merseyside on another of her rare peregrinations, this time flying the Portuguese flag and bound for Madeira where she had been chartered to commence a new ferry service between Funchal, Madeira and Porto Santo. Porto Santo is a small holiday island with a huge military runway which is also used by all commercial flights from Madeira for refuelling. The flight from Madeira to Porto Santo lasts just eight minutes and is the shortest scheduled airline flight in the world! The Island has 5,000 inhabitants and travel by sea involves a voyage of about 40 miles. She was also scheduled to make several 200 mile trips to the Canary Islands.

The author feels he may have some vicarious responsibility for this chain of events. When he was in Madeira five years ago, upon seeing the so called fast craft then operating to Porto Santo, wallowing helplessly in the Atlantic swell just outside his hotel bedroom window, the author commented that the then recently idle ***Mona's Queen*** could be well employed thus. Many a true word! *A selection of photographs of the "Lady's" Madeira interlude appears on page 121.*

One significant alteration that had to be made to the "Lady" to equip her for work in the Atlantic was the fitting of a watertight door on the vehicle ramp thus sealing off the car deck. The rationale for this being that in Irish Sea service, even in the worst seas ever encountered it would never be possible for a large enough sea to build up and engulf the ship from astern. However in the Atlantic where the height of waves, distance between them and the fetch can be massive, it was considered possible that the ***Lady of Mann*** could find herself in exceptional conditions. In the extreme, these seas could break over the stern of the ship and as she was pooped, the water could have found its way down onto the vehicle deck making her liable to capsize. Upon her return to the Irish Sea, the unnecessary watertight door was removed as it restricted access to the main car deck.

While the ***Lady of Mann*** was away in Madeira, the Steam Packet Company's flagship ***King Orry*** had to go into dry-dock for repairs to her bowthruster, scheduled to take three days. While she was off service it was intended that the ***Seacat Isle of Man*** would deputise for her following the closing of her own summer seasons sailings. It was well known that the SeaCat was not suitable for rough weather work and the best the Company could hope for was that the Irish Sea would remain kind for the three day extension to her season. However this was not to be and her final sailing outwards on 27th September 1995 had to be diverted from Heysham to Liverpool because of gales. There followed a most unfortunate few hours when the SeaCat remained stormbound at Liverpool. Belatedly, she tried in vain to leave the Mersey and return her weary passengers to the Island but after a short while she encountered heavy seas off Formby and was seriously damaged in the process. Her master wisely decided that enough was enough and returned to Liverpool. The SeaCat was laid up, somewhat battered and proven to be unsuitable for winter work in the Irish Sea. This reflects no criticism whatsoever of the vessel which had very many good points. But, just as the ***Lady of Mann's*** "Achilles Heel" was her lack of freight capacity, the SeaCat's inability to sustain a reliable service in heavy seas (which are common enough in then Irish Sea) was, along with her great cost, to be her downfall.

The ***Lady of Mann*** ended her charter to Madeira on 13th November 1995 and returned to Birkenhead, arriving in the early hours of the 16th November when she entered Cammell Laird's basin for refit.

Finally, after five years being idle and awaiting a buyer, the ***Mona's Queen*** was sold to "Filipino business interests" for an undisclosed sum described by the Steam Packet Company as "a modest premium over book value". She had been renamed ***Mary The Queen*** and left Birkenhead for the long delivery voyage with three Steam Packet engineers aboard on 4th December 1995. *Two excellent photographs by Gordon Ditchfield appear on page 124.* She was expected to take about three weeks for the passage which was routed via Malta, Suez, Columbo and Singapore for refuelling stops. For a ship designed for

This series of photographs shows the **Lady of Mann** *saying farewell to her home port, Douglas, on 28th June 1994. With Capt. Kinley in command, dressed overall and siren blowing mournfully, the ship went astern from the No. 2 berth on the Victoria Pier, turned in the outer harbour and sailed slowly northwards towards Onchan before turning again and sailing past the harbour entrance prior to disappearing into the dawn. The whole scene was redolent of 17th August 1971 when her old namesake, the first* **Lady of Mann** *with Capt. Tom Corteen in command, left Douglas for the last time.* *(photos: Author)*

Charter in Madeira

Left: A brilliantly emotive photograph taken on 17th July 1995 (by ship lover and former Cammell Laird man Peter Stewart) of the **Lady of Mann** *re-registered in Madeira and setting sail for Funchal. Seen against the backdrop of the wonderful Liverpool waterfront that had been her second home for almost twenty years, when she left Merseyside, the concern was that she might never come back again. (photo: Peter Stewart)*

Above: The **Lady of Mann** *alongside at Porto Santo.*
(photo: IOMSPC)

Above: The watertight door fitted to the **Lady of Mann's** *vehicle ramp for use when operating in the Atlantic.*
(photo: IOMSPC)

Left: The **Lady of Mann** *alongside at Funchal*
(photo: Jack Ronan collection)

normal journeys of 4 hours duration, the voyage must rank as one of the more challenging!

After much discussion, in July 1995, the third of the Douglas linkspans was commissioned, this one owned by the Government. They then entered into what became known as the "Linkspan User Agreement" with the Steam Packet Company which was described as something of a compromise. In return for what in practise amounted to a government approved virtual monopoly of roll on-roll off shipping services to the Island, the Steam Packet Company had to guarantee levels of service, off-island advertising, fleet investment and fares price stability etc.

Whilst the Steam Packet Company had the option to renew its charter of the SeaCat for another year, the Island's tourist industry was stunned to hear at the end of 1995 that the fast craft service would not be continued in 1996 and that the seasonal routes would once again be operated by the ***Lady of Mann***. Tynwald, the Isle of Man Government set up a Select Committee to look into all aspects of the shock announcement and has been taking evidence since.

In all but the worst weather, the operations of the SeaCat were greatly appreciated by passengers and the tourist business generally. This was because the vessel travelled at speeds of 35 knots which virtually halved standard crossing times and enabled several trips per day to be made, at times which were likely to suit everyone.

Despite all this in her favour, the cruel fact is that she was not a financial success and, other than some additional day trippers, failed to generate significantly more business for the Company despite her huge expense. The SeaCat cost much more to charter, more to operate and more in maintenance than a conventional craft of similar capacity. Also, first generation high speed craft such as the ***Seacat Isle of Man*** were not built for rough weather and in adverse conditions the incidence of seasickness could be very high indeed. Whilst the latter was never cited as a reason for withdrawing the service, it was clearly always going to be an unfortunate problem in poor weather.

Despite having had to withdraw the SeaCat the Steam Packet Company have said that high speed craft are the answer for the Isle of Man trade but they acknowledge that a faster and more substantially built craft is required if it is to be able to operate in anything other than calm weather. Fleet engineer Michael Casey is not alone in the Company in having spent considerable time and effort evaluating all aspects of fast craft for use on Manx sea routes and there is no doubt that his and others' considerable experience and devotion to solving the equation will, in due time, bear fruit.

To enable the ***King Orry*** to receive routine annual overhaul and survey, the ***Lady of Mann*** vacated dock at Birkenhead on the afternoon of 8th February 1996 and crossed light (empty) to Douglas where she arrived at around 17.00 berthing at the No.2 berth on the south side of the Victoria Pier. Normally the ***Lady of Mann*** berths on the north side of the pier but storm force winds were forecast for that night and the next day, so some shelter was afforded by berthing inside the harbour. The ***King Orry*** duly arrived from Heysham shortly after the ***Lady of Mann*** had docked, and berthed as usual at the linkspan. Some stores and other supplies were transferred from the ***King Orry*** to the ***Lady of Mann*** and the ***King Orry*** was then able to stand down. The ***Lady of Mann*** resumed sailings on her native Irish Sea route with the day return sailing from Douglas to Liverpool on Saturday 10th February 1996 as the previous days storms caused her sailings to be cancelled.

In his statement dated 25th March 1996 which accompanied the 1995 preliminary results of the Company, Steam Packet Chairman Mr. J H (Juan) Kelly outlined why the financial results were so disappointing.

Clearly, the losses made on the abortive North Sea freight service using the ***Belard*** (which the company bought for the specific purpose) had made big inroads into profitability.

The operation of the SeaCat was stated as being responsible for a further £2 million reduction in profitability.

Talking of future fleet operations, he went on to say " We believe that this can be achieved by moving to a fleet comprising a large passenger/freight ship operating all year round and a suitable high speed craft operating for perhaps eight months from March to October each year".

"As I write, we are well advanced with our planning in respect of the replacement vessels and our aim is to have these in service by 1998. 1995 was a disappointing year, but the causes of this disappointment will not be repeated. Having "cleared the decks" your board look forward with great confidence to a successful 1996 and a profitable future operation, based on a new fleet fit for the new millennium". In a radio news interview that followed, Mr Kelly confirmed that they would keep a suitable ship in reserve and suggested that the existing freight ro-ro ship ***Peveril*** (built twenty-five years ago) might be retained for the purpose.

On 29th March 1996, just four days after the chairman's statement, came the unexpected news that the Isle of Man Steam Packet Company had been taken-over by Mr. Jim Sherwood's Sea Containers.

Readers of the author's earlier books will note that in the September 1990 foreword to his work entitled *The Isle of Man*

Steam Packet, Volume 2 which by then had sold out and, reprinted, ran to a second edition, there had already been a previous take-over attempt by Mr. Sherwood on 25th June that year.

The latest Sea Containers' offer to acquire the whole of the remainder of the Steam Packet Company followed their announcement that a further 4,371,651 shares had been acquired giving them over 58% anyway.

The same afternoon, Sea Containers' president, Mr Jim Sherwood travelled to the Isle of Man for talks with Chief Minister, Mr Miles Walker and to assure him that employment, services and the future operations of the company were all safe in his hands.

He went on to state the background to and reasons for the take over offer.

"Sea Containers has decided to take a controlling interest in the Steam Packet Company because of its belief in the potential of the business and its view that its other ferry and port interests in the Irish Sea could be consolidated to the benefit of both the Steam Packet Company and Sea Containers. The use of high speed car ferry services in the Irish Sea is increasing bringing Liverpool, Blackpool, Belfast and Dublin markets closer to the Isle of Man by cutting travel time almost in half. Sea Containers intends to provide two high speed ferries, one of which would operate year round and a 21 knot freight vessel with adequate passenger accommodation which could also serve other Irish Sea ports besides Heysham and Douglas in order to take the Steam Packet Company into its next stage of development".

The statement continued "Following the offer, Sea Containers intends to invite Mr Juan Kelly to continue as non-executive chairman of the Steam Packet Company. It is expected that Mr. David Dixon and Mr. Brett Martin will both leave the Steam Packet Group shortly after the Annual General Meeting on 2nd May 1996. It is intended to appoint Mr. Hamish Ross, currently a non-executive director as Managing Director of the Steam Packet Company. Mr Ross currently manages Sea Containers' existing Irish Sea interests including the Stranraer-Larne SeaCat service and the Port of Heysham".

So what does the future hold for the Isle of Man Steam Packet Company and its fleet? From Mr Jim Sherwood's statements, we know that by 1998, all three existing ships will be withdrawn and replaced by an entirely new fleet comprising a new passenger carrying freighter and two fast craft. If this happens he will have done in two years, what, for different reasons, took thirty to achieve following the end of the Second World War.

The ro-ro freighter ***Peveril*** has seen many different geographic areas of operations since her building in Norway in 1971 as the ***Holmia*** for Silja Line's service across the Baltic Sea. She was acquired by the Steam Packet Company in 1981 and has been the backbone of the company's freight ro-ro service ever since.

The ***King Orry*** began life as a train ferry named ***Saint Eloi*** and at that time, she was owned by A.L.A., (Societe Anonyme de Navigation Angleterre-Lorraine-Alsace) a subsidiary of British Railways, International and Shipping Services Division, later to change its name to Sealink (U.K.) Limited. She carried the A.L.A. logo on her funnel rather than the double arrow device of the rest of the main railway owned fleet. Whilst she was ordered in 1969 and was launched in 1972, her builders, Cantiere Navale di Pietra, of Ligure, Genoa, Italy, then went into liquidation and there followed protracted negotiations with creditors to try to get the ship completed and handed over. Finally, she was completed and commenced commercial train ferry operations from Dover to Dunkerque in 1975. Towards the end of her career in the south, she ceased carrying passengers and railway traffic and for a while carried road freight only.

By the time she was acquired by the Steam Packet Company on Valentines Day, 1990, she had been renamed ***Channel Entente*** and named thus, she entered Manx Service complete with much evidence of railway track on her vehicle deck as if to remind travellers that she really was a train ferry. During her autumn refit later that year, she was renamed ***King Orry.***

Both the ***Peveril*** and the ***King Orry*** are now getting on in years but upon their disposal from Manx shipping routes under Sea Containers' control, will certainly find buyers and further work.

The ***Lady of Mann*** is the last remaining Manx passenger ship that has her origins rooted in the era that began at the end of the War. When it came to carrying passengers, the Steam Packet Company were very much in the "volume" business, their ships being licensed to carry more than all others. At that time, the late 1940s, all coastal shipping was still regulated under licence granted by the British Ministry of Transport, passports and identity cards were needed for travel to Northern and Southern Ireland. The Isle of Man Steam Packet Company still had a substantial interest in Isle of Man Airways and Steam Packet Company deliveries were made by horse drawn wagons! The tourist industry's own body was known by the grand sounding title "The Isle of Man Visiting Industry and Catering Association" whilst today's Department of Tourism and Leisure was known simply as the Isle of Man Publicity Board. A little later, local airlines including Isle of Man Airways were grouped up and sold to British European Airways.

In the thirty years that followed the war, the Steam Packet Company rebuilt its fleet completely. Mostly, those new ships were paid for out of revenue generated funds; bluntly, cash at

The **Mona's Queen**, *rust streaked and looking very tired, was renamed* **Mary The Queen** *when she was sold after being laid up awaiting a buyer for over five years. These two historic photographs by the author's friend of long standing, Gordon Ditchfield, taken the day before she departed, show the rather amateur signwriting attempt that had indicated the ship's change of name and port of registry.*

(photos: Gordon Ditchfield)

the top of the pile, money in the bank. More recently, with the exception of the ***Belard***, large marine mortgages were necessary to help spread the cost of new acquisitions which has made long term financial and strategic planning far more critical.

The ***Lady of Mann*** is approaching middle age. She is now over twenty years old but she carries her maturity well. Fresh from overhaul and survey, she looks resplendent in the time honoured Steam Packet livery. She is utterly reliable in storm and calm weather and is perfectly capable of fast passages. She will operate on all Manx routes during 1996 and perhaps beyond?

When the sad day comes and she finally becomes redundant here, it can only be a matter of speculation as to where she might find further work. The market for such ships without roll on-roll off freight capacity is quite small and to pioneer a new route where there is not yet even a linkspan would be something of a commercial gamble. On the other hand, there are still routes around the world where her design features would make her the ideal people and car carrier.

Whilst the ***Manx Maid*** and the ***Ben-my-Chree*** were rather optimistically described by the Steam Packet Company Chairman as "still having some useful life in them" when they were withdrawn in 1984, being steam powered and restricted to passengers and light vehicles only, sad though it was, it came as no great surprise to see them prematurely scrapped.

The ***Mona's Queen***, which took five years to sell, was more modern in concept and had diesel powered machinery but was still designed especially for the Manx, mainly tourist oriented trade.

The ***Lady of Mann*** is an altogether better proposition being newer in all respects, not just in terms of physical age. Her main engines are far more powerful than the others' and are in first class order. Following her major rebuilding in 1989, vehicle capacity is a very creditable 130 or more cars or light vans (but she cannot carry heavy goods vehicles). Passenger accommodation is well appointed but becomes somewhat limited for space on the occasions that it is necessary for her to sail with more than say, 500 passengers aboard.

What must be said is that she is a fine ship, operated by a company with the longest of all service records and manned by the best officers and crew afloat. In their day, the construction of the four side-loading car ferries probably did more to aid the Isle of Man and its economic revival than any other maritime event. For this we all owe a great debt of gratitude to the men of vision that made that all-important decision back in 1959.

Let us hope that the opportunity for longevity will be afforded to the ***Lady of Mann*** and that wherever she sails, her future will be bright for many years to come.

This book, *So Strong and So Fair,* started out as an appreciation of the four side-loading car ferries of the Isle of Man Steam Packet Company and some of the people associated with them. Following the Sea Containers' take-over announcement on 29th March 1996, to some readers the book will have taken on the hallmarks of a valedictory and even a eulogy. Many of us, not least the author, grieve the passing of the old era.

In 1961, before the arrival of the first car ferry, the Steam Packet Company carried 10,561 cars and 15,259 motorcycles to the Island. By 1972, the number of cars carried had risen to over 49,000 whilst the motorcycle business remained unchanged. Later still, with four car ferries in operation in 1984, the number of cars had risen yet again to almost 60,000 and over 19,000 motorcycles were carried. From then onwards and some would say belatedly, following the merger with Sealink/Manx Line, the nature of the business changed fundamentally from being very much a service industry to the Island's tourist trade, to one driven by pure commerciality.

But that, we are taught to believe, is the inevitable result of economic progress. Perhaps, if that fundamental change had occurred earlier, rather than being resisted until 1985, the future would have turned out entirely differently?

With the take-over announcement by Sea Containers very fresh in peoples' minds it would be understandable if the announcement is looked upon completely negatively.

The uncertainty alone will be sufficient to upset many.

Indeed, supporters of the "old" Steam Packet Company will see the announcement as very much the end of a long and often rough voyage and from many perfectly correct points of view, that is certainly the case.

However, setting aside the all understandable worry and sadness, there is an important and positive side to all this and in time, the Island will settle down with the new owner of its main shipping services and hopefully be able to reap the benefits. In short, the Island has to have faith, perhaps plenty of it, in the final outcome that may not be known for years to come.

Mr. Jim Sherwood is renowned for making a success of his business ventures and there is good reason to believe that the Isle of Man Steam Packet Company under Sea Containers' control will prosper to the advantage of all concerned.

In return for the Manx people's faith, it is to be hoped, perhaps even expected, that Mr. Jim Sherwood will look kindly upon the Steam Packet Company's great history and that he will take steps to ensure that under his stewardship, that history continues to grow, well into the future.

The incomparable **Lady of Mann.** *Together with her sisters, they did so much for the Isle of Man!* *(photo: Author)*

Author's Thanks and Acknowledgements

The author regards himself as privileged to have been so close to the people and the ships of the Isle of Man Steam Packet Company. When he made his first trip to the Isle of Man back in 1956 at the age of ten, little did he know that, fifteen years later, Laxey was to become the family home.

Even at that young age, the author's passion for excursion ships, ferries and cross channel steamers was well established, his first written works on the subject dated July 1954 remain a treasured family possession.

The author's father, George, himself a former deep sea marine radio officer, later Head of Radio and Telecommunications at the main London College and author of marine radio manuals, had a long association with Marconi Marine. In that connection, from a very young age the author was able to make frequent visits to Britain's ports and harbours visiting liners and ferries at every opportunity. This provided an ideal spawning ground for what has remained his lifelong interest and hobby.

The author would like to place on record his grateful thanks to a number of people who have helped to make this book a reality.

Firstly, thanks go to the author's father for enthusiastically passing on his own love of ships and the sea and for all the opportunities the mutual interest had presented over the years.

Secondly, to Ray Pugh of Southport who has been a valued friend and correspondent of the author for a very long time.

Both of the gentlemen, now well into their 80s have brought a wealth of photographic and marine knowledge, not only to these proceedings but also to all the author's previous literary and journalistic efforts.

Ray Pugh's sister Barbara and nephew Gordon Ditchfield have helped greatly to complete the family contribution over many years without which help and friendship the author's tasks would have been all the harder.

Individual photographers' work is gratefully acknowledged and their names are shown herein, next to their photographs. Over the years a number of first class photographers, friends and others well known to the author have been very generous in allowing access to their superb collections. Amongst these are David Parsons, John Collins, Noel Howarth, Eddie Fryer, Gordon Ditchfield, the late Bill Peters and John Nicholson.

Contributors of anecdotal information have assisted tremendously and their contributions help to transform the book from a series of cold facts into something, hopefully more light hearted and personal.

Captain Jack Ronan, a man of great nautical experience and tradition, has been notable in his enthusiasm and willingness to provide every possible assistance as well as much valuable time for meetings and written details.

Captain Harry Kinley has also allowed the author to draw generously upon his experiences and knowledge of life in the Isle of Man Steam Packet Company.

John Clarke, Harry Kefford, Trevor Skillicorn have contributed in very practical ways allowing the author to discuss their particular interests with them or writing in detail of their experiences.

One of the great privileges when writing thanks and acknowledgements is to be able to mention with pride and affection the friendship extended by our great sea captains, now sadly no longer with us. Captain Westby Kissack, Captain Ernie McMeiken (often referred to as "Hurricane Mac" on account of his love of gales), Captain Tom Corteen and Captain Harvey Collister were four top men whose assistance and comradeship the author will always remember. Phyllis Kissack and Vera McMeiken have both helped in the production of this work and the author wishes to express his thanks for their willingness to talk and for the use of scrapbooks and memoirs.

Whilst researching his contribution to a new Economic History of the Isle of Man being compiled under the aegis of The Centre for Manx Studies (founded by the University of Liverpool and the Isle of Man Government and Manx National Heritage), the author was granted wide access to historic detailed proceedings of the directors of the Isle of Man Steam Packet Company. With the specific permission of the present managing director, Mr D. Dixon, some of those interesting details appear in this book and the author wishes to extend his thanks to David Dixon and Phil Watterson, the Registrar, for their faith in these endeavours.

Finally, if through inadvertence the author has failed to name, recognise or acknowledge individually any efforts past or present that have enabled this work to come to fruition, he now does so wholeheartedly and unreservedly.

Above: On arrival at Liverpool on 26th January 1991, a bitterly cold day with a crisp frost and hoariness everywhere, Capt. Edward Fargher, the fleet commodore, had to rouse the skipper of the tug **Brackengarth** *which was berthed on the Landing Stage in the way of the* **Lady of Mann.** *Several explosive blasts on the ship's siren soon had the tug master running along the Landing Stage to move his tug!* *(photo: Author)*

Right: 23rd June 1990 is the date for this scene. The **Lady of Mann** *is seen passing Perch Rock, New Brighton at the entrance to the River Mersey, inward bound from the Isle of Man. There is a gale blowing and it being high water adds to the spectacle.*
The author spent all his childhood holidays in and around Liverpool and other major British ports in the 1950s and 1960s prior to coming to live in the Isle of Man twenty-five years ago. The long periods spent on Merseyside were the inspiration for an earlier very successful book by the author (now sadly out of print) entitled The Mighty Mersey and its Ferries. *(photo: Author)*